"Mike Mack's book should be read and studied by anyone in the church interested in assimilating and growing believers! He is a veteran of small group ministry and knows how to help people grow in their faith. I highly recommend this work to leaders and lay people, as well."
- Dr. David Roadcup, Executive Director, Center for Church Advancement Cincinnati Christian University

"Finally! A book about small groups to help us decide we should have small groups and to know whether our small groups are fulfilling a biblical purpose. Although this book is practical, it is refreshingly devoid of self-centered trendiness."
- Mark A. Taylor, Editor and Publisher, *Christian Standard*

"There are certain questions that keep me up at night. 'Is my small group really healthy?' happens to be one of them. I am not shooting for a 'good' small group, but a 'great' one that is a God-centered reflection of who and what He intends small groups to be. I'm so indebted for *Small Group Vital Signs*. It's helping me ensure m
- Ben Reed, Community Groups

"Deming taught in business that if y   as a process, you don't know what you are doing. For forty years   is been challenged to figure out the process of making disciples and I love that everywhere you look, churches get it and real disciples are being made. Mike Mack gets it and he is doing it every day at his church. He has also been around a long time and watched the small group movement grow and flourish. Read this book and you'll also know what you're doing."
- Boyd Pelley, Co-founder/President, Churchteams

"The only people who should not read *Small Group Vital Signs* are those who love to sit home in the dark-by themselves or are addicted to mediocrity. For everyone else, get ready for a tune-up and an upgrade!"
- Thom Corrigan, author of *101 Great Ideas to Create a Caring Group*

"It's easy to meander along and just assume that everything's fine with our group. But how do we know for sure? In *Small Group Vital Signs*, Mike offers a thorough discussion on each of the seven vital signs. Mike is a shepherd at heart. If your group seems to be lacking something, but you're not sure what, you'll benefit from this book."
- Pat Sikora, Author, *Why Didn't You Warn Me?*

"Don't mess around. If you want to lead a healthy small group—if you want to see healthy small groups in your church—you need to read this book."
- Sam O'Neal, content editor for *Threads* by LifeWay

"Don't settle for the status quo! Mike Mack's *Small Group Vital Signs* will not only gauge the current health and vitality of your groups, but give you a growth plan for helping them grow and reproduce."
- Jon Ferguson, Community Christian Church

"As I read this book, I was inspired, encouraged, and challenged as a small group pastor to refocus my efforts to build a small group ministry that embodies the essence of biblical community, to be the Body of Christ."
- Randy Boschee, Life Groups Pastor, Liquid Church

"Small Groups aren't the answer. Healthy small groups are. Michael Mack has written the kind of book that you can read today and put into practice tomorrow."
-Adam Workman, Small Group Pastor, LifePoint Church

"Michael Mack certainly knows his stuff. In *Small Group Vital Signs* he skillfully blends his passion with solid content and practical wisdom. I really, *really* like this book and plan on using it as a core text in training our small group leaders."
- Dave Earley, Pastor, Grace City Church
and author of *8 Habits of Effective Small Group Leaders*

"What a fantastic contribution to the small group world. Michael Mack's strong theological framework and unrelenting emphasis on the importance of a Christ-centered and spiritually healthy group leader is the launching point to authentic community."
- Rick Zeiger, Small Group Area Pastor, Saddleback Church

For the body of Christ to function as it was designed, we need to give ourselves regular check-ups. *Small Group Vital Signs* clears away a lot of the clutter that has clouded our understanding of building healthy community and moves us back to the priority of centering our lives around Christ.
- Heather Zempel, Discipleship Pastor, National Community Church
Author, *Sacred Roads* and *Community is Messy*

"Without a doubt, this is one of the most important books you will ever read if you're determined to experience powerful, transformational, and authentic biblical community. Mike has done a brilliant job of contrasting the difference between a man-made group and a Christ-centered group!"
- Dr. Ralph W. Neighbour, Jr., author, pastor,
and consultant to the global cell movement

SMALL GROUP VITAL SIGNS

SEVEN INDICATORS OF HEALTH
THAT MAKE GROUPS FLOURISH

BY MICHAEL C. MACK

TOUCH Publications, Inc
Houston, Texas

SMALL GROUP VITAL SIGNS

SEVEN
INDICATORS
OF HEALTH
THAT MAKE
GROUPS
FLOURISH

MICHAEL C. MACK

Published by TOUCH Publications, Inc.
P.O. Box 7847, Houston, Texas 77270 USA
800-735-5865 • www.touchusa.org

Printed in the United States of America

Cover design: www.neubauerdesign.com
Editor: Randall G. Neighbour

International Standard Book Number: 978-0-9825352-5-7

All scripture quotations, unless otherwise indicated,
are from the Holy Bible, New International Version,
Copyright © 1973, 1978, 1984 by International Bible Society.
Used with permission.

TOUCH Publications is the book-publishing division of TOUCH
Outreach Ministries, a resource and consulting ministry for churches
with a vision for healthy small groups.

DEDICATION

"For the Lamb at the center of the throne will be their
shepherd; he will lead them to springs of living water."
Revelation 7:17

This book is dedicated to Jesus. Thank you for being my Lamb, Good Shepherd, and the center of my life. May You use this book to lead every group to You, our Living Water.

May You be at the center of each group who reads it, and may these pages put a smile on Your face and bring You glory.

ACKNOWLEDGEMENTS

This book is a group effort! Hundreds of people over the years have influenced my thinking about what makes a small group healthy. Some are mentioned in these pages.

While I cannot mention everyone, I'd like to especially acknowledge Murphy Belding, who partnered with me at Northeast as we initiated the development of the seven vital signs; the small group leaders at Northeast who provided input on these vital signs, worked through the initial assessment, and committed to the health of their groups; and Jerry Anderson, a leader at our church who helped me refine the assessment questions.

Finally, a big thanks to Randall Neighbour, who tirelessly chopped, improved, revised, and provided lots of feedback and ideas along the way. His partnership on this book was invaluable!

TABLE OF CONTENTS

I am awestruck by Mike's ability to take us to the right places. I know they are the right places because Mike has been on the journey himself and is simply showing us where to tread.

As I made my way through this astoundingly insightful read, I found myself questioning so many aspects of group life that I have embraced and taught on over the years. I wondered if I helped groups to depend enough on the power of the Holy Spirit, the presence of Christ, and the strength of God the Father. I pondered how many small group ministries are over the top when it comes to teaching techniques, but lacking in helping small group leaders and coaches determine when to set aside "the right thing to do" with "the right way to think." I questioned the discipleship models I have so often espoused and asked myself if they were the way Jesus discipled His followers. I even asked myself this question: "Did the small group movement deteriorate and embrace principles and practices birthed in a psychology class while setting aside principles and practices birthed in the heart of God and revealed in His Word?"

Most small group books tell you why, how, or what the author has done or is doing in his church. While reading these books, I thought, "You told me why, now tell me how" … or "You told me how, now tell me why" … or "You told me what you are doing, but will it work in *any* setting with *any* demographic?" One of the most refreshing things about this book is that Mike puts all three of the puzzle pieces in place. But most importantly, everything—and I do mean *everything*—is proven true via Scripture. And when Scripture speaks, the principles and practices are universal.

As you use the health assessment and then read this book, my prayer is that you set aside past paradigms to consider what I see as the heart of this book: God will do something amazing in the life of any group that gives Him room to do so.

Mike, thank you for taking your time to give the small group world a resource that will help us see a biblical small group within walking distance of every person on the planet.

— Rick Howerton, Global Small Group Environmentalist for
NavPress and author of *A New Kind of Tribe*

FOREWORD

Small groups are part of life. I cannot remember a time in my life where there was not some form of small group. From the Kindergarten classroom organization, to lunchroom experience where we sought out the place where "my" people sat, to team sports . . . small groups are everywhere.

And from my experience they were always a part of church life too. It just happened in what we called Sunday school. We also had home Bible studies and committees. Because small groups are part of the warp and woof of how good living works, it's only natural that the church would get stuff done in and through small groups.

With the focus on the centrality of small groups over the last 20 years, they have moved beyond just being a natural way of organizing activities as in the church of my childhood. Now they form the base of church operations. We are truly seeing the reality of what it means to be a church *of* small groups and not just a church *with* small groups.

But this question remains: What are we experiencing?

That's where the book you are now reading steps up to the plate. It's as if the bases are loaded. We've gained a clear understanding of our need for community on third base. On second, we've got excellent structures to organize group life and train leaders. On first, we have thousands of group leaders in churches all across North America. And up to bat is Mike's encouragement to focus on seven important aspects of healthy group life. If the wisdom and experience found here is heeded, it will drive in all those runners. Grand Slam!

The church deserves more than people gathering in living rooms every week. We need people who live out healthy missional living, which this book describes. *Small Group Vital Signs* is more than a strategy manual. It's a life manual that can make all the difference in the way God's Kingdom is revealed in your neighborhood.

— Scott Boren, Director, The Center for Community and Mission and author of *MissioRelate* and *Missional Small Groups*

PREFACE

For a small group to remain powerful for God's kingdom and life changing for the members, every small group leader should ask himself or herself some tough questions:

"Is my small group healthy?"
"Is my group thriving, surviving, or declining?"
"Is my group in missional or maintenance mode?"

These are excellent questions. However, they raise a few more: How do you know if your group is healthy or not? How are you gauging the vitality of your small group?

Much of the time, leaders just make assumptions, go with a gut feeling, compare their group to another group, or just don't care. The truth is that small groups are too important to God and everyone involved to gauge health on wishful thinking, poor comparisons, or a "whatever" attitude.

In my role as a small groups pastor, I wanted to know if the small groups at my church were healthy, and our lead pastor wanted to know as well. Neither of us wanted to make uneducated guesses or assumptions. And, more significantly, we wanted a solid growth plan for helping our groups become as healthy, vibrant, and strong as they could be. Last year, we surveyed all our small groups in order to coach and equip them based on the results. This took months of planning and follow-up.

You may be asking yourself, "Why go to all the trouble to conduct a survey and analyze data on top of everything else going on in the small group ministry?" We did all this because God created the world in such a way that healthy things grow and reproduce themselves.

> Healthy things grow.
> Growing things change.
> Change challenges us.
> Challenges cause us to
> trust God. Trust leads to
> obedience. Obedience
> makes us healthy.
> And healthy things grow.[1]

As a small group minister, coach, and consultant, I've noticed that many groups in churches all over America are not growing or reproducing. When I see or hear about lackluster groups, I always think, "Why do many small groups settle for average or 'just good-enough' meetings led by ordinary leaders who have a listless spiritual life?" I can only imagine you understand what I'm referring to here. These are groups that have a typical Bible study on comfy couches, while the members engage in the usual and expected conversations about the text. Truth be told, many small groups have drifted into mediocrity and have settled in as a "nice little group" for armchair Christians.

Stop and think about this "nice little group." As I've described it, does it sound like something your next-door neighbor would want to join? Will a group like this make a big impact on our world? I don't think so. Stagnant, plateaued, and narcissistic groups are not healthy and they don't create an environment for life transformation. They will not change the world. And worst of all, they dishonor God.

This is the main reason I wrote this book. I believe God can and will use healthy small group communities to change the world, one life at a time. But this will not go unopposed. One of Satan's main strategies is to convince Christians to play it safe, settle for unexceptional results, and aim for comfort. I don't want to see small groups give in to Satan's corruption and watered down schemes, and I hope you feel the same way.

In the pages that follow, I've outlined a God-given battle plan for helping your group become healthy so you can move out on mission together and live a powerful, exceptional life in Christ.

This is a war for souls . . . our souls and millions who don't yet know Christ as Lord. It's time to ask hard questions about our groups, make changes, and thereby harness the power of biblical community to send Satan's minions back to hell with their tails between their legs.

INTRODUCTION:
Small Group Charades

One evening, I began our small group meeting with a big question, "Why does our small group exist?" Before I gave anyone a chance to respond, I told my group our icebreaker for the evening was to play a game of charades. Then, we discussed three Scripture passages from *The Message*, examining each one to help us better answer my opening question:

Hosea 6:6 - I'm after love that lasts, not more religion. I want you to know God, not go to more prayer meetings.

Amos 5:21-24 - I can't stand your religious meetings. I'm fed up with your conferences and conventions. I want nothing to do with your religion projects, your pretentious slogans and goals. I'm sick of your fund-raising schemes, your public relations and image making. I've had all I can take of your noisy ego-music. When was the last time you sang to me? Do you know what I want? I want justice—oceans of it. I want fairness—rivers of it. That's what I want. That's all I want.

Isaiah 1:13-17 - Quit your worship charades. I can't stand your trivial religious games: Monthly conferences, weekly Sabbaths, special meetings—meetings, meetings, meetings—I can't stand one more! Meetings for this, meetings for that. I hate them! You've worn me out! I'm sick of your religion, religion, religion, while you go right on sinning. When you put on your next prayer-performance, I'll be looking the other way. No matter how long or loud or often you pray, I'll not be listening. And do you know why? Because you've been tearing people to pieces, and your hands are bloody. Go home and wash up. Clean up your act. Sweep your lives clean of your evil doings so I don't have to look at them any longer. Say no to wrong. Learn to do good. Work for justice. Help the down-and-out. Stand up for the homeless. Go to bat for the defenseless.

To help my group members answer my initial, big-picture question, we discussed three easier questions that helped us think differently about our small group and its reason to exist:

1. According to these passages, what does God *not* want?
2. What *does* God want? What is he pleased with?
3. What can we learn from these Scriptures as we plan for group life this fall?

Together, we discovered the following:
- God is not satisfied with small group meeting and weekend service attendance alone.
- A healthy small group is about loving God and one another, including those outside our groups.
- A healthy small group is about living for God and carrying out Christ's mission.
- A healthy small group is about justice and mercy for outsiders, not just another gathering for insiders.
- A healthy small group is comprised of *real* people in *real* relationships making a *real* difference.

In other words, healthy small groups don't play "small group charades!"

"No matter how many people attend religious meetings [small groups], if the result is not obedience to God and concern for our neighbor, the meetings are a failure." [1]

How We Got Here

I've become a student of the history of small groups in the United States. I've also read most every book published on the topic of small group ministry. From what I've learned, the meeting-mindedness that defines small group ministry in North America is a consequence of many years of programmatic systems and methods that have been put in place over the last several decades. But it wasn't always this way.

The small group movement was birthed in several para-church organizations in the 70s (Alcoholics Anonymous and college campus ministries) and a handful of daring congregations led by visionary lead pastors. These ministries had a built-in relationality that allowed small group life to flourish. When the *program* of small groups was moved into traditional church structures, the heart of strongly bonded relational ties was missing. Small group ministry was adopted and used by church growth gurus during the 80s and 90s as a way of closing the back door of the church.

Today, there's a new trend in writing and speaking about small groups, and it is very good! Titles like *Simple Small Groups*, *Organic Community*, and *The Relational Way* are now on bookshelves. Pastors and writers are using words like *holistic* when discussing small groups ministry. It's plain to see that the Western church is attempting to transition away from a program-based design to a more simple, relational, organic movement. While it will be difficult to transform an institutionalized, entrenched system into something that seems so radical and revolutionary as restoring redemptive relationships, I believe it can be done.

This is truly a restoration to the church as Jesus envisioned it. We are part of a church movement that desires to restore New Testament Christianity. In my opinion, of all the areas needing restoration, the greatest is the value of *relational living*. If we get this right, everything else will fall in place naturally.

Jesus faced this same difficulty with the Pharisees, who focused on the institution of their religion (the temple), their culture and history, and their rules (programs for how to live like a good Jew). But they missed out on the most important aspect . . . a relationship with Jesus! Peter and John continued to struggle with these same institutionalized leaders. Then, the Holy Spirit moved in and through these men to radically change their worlds. I believe the same thing can and will happen today.

It's fascinating to me that the Holy Spirit did not inspire New Testament writers to give us methods or systems for doing small group ministry. Instead, we see instructions for how to *be* the church; live together in the body of Christ, and successfully reach a world that needs God and biblical community.

While I'm sure it would sell better, this book does not contain "seven practices for small group success," nor is it a "how-to guide" to involve 100% of your church's congregation in a small group program. Instead, it's about the simple, *relational* vital signs that will transform any small group into something God will use to radically change our churches, our neighborhoods, our workplaces, our world, and us!

A Healthy Group Is the Body of Christ

At its core, a small group is Christ's body in action. Stop and think about this for a moment. Your small group *is* the church. Not a subset of the church. Not a supportive program within the church. Not a tool to close the back door. Unfortunately, in today's world, our mental image of "church" is usually something much bigger or more institutional than a single small group. We say, "I'm going to church," meaning a building, a mass meeting, or possibly a structured program of some sort. The New Testament never uses the word *church* that way. Rather it refers to God's people, called to carry out his mission.[2] The New Testament uses the word *church* in three basic ways:

1. The church that meets in the home (Romans 16:5; 1 Corinthians 16:19; Philemon 1:2)
2. The church in a certain geographical area (Acts 13:1; Romans 16:1; 1 Corinthians 1:2)
3. All of God's called-out people (*ecclesia*, Matthew 16:18)

My objective here is not to get into a pointless argument about the definition of words (see 1 Timothy 6:4 and 2 Timothy 2:14). I want to help you see what your group *really* is, or at least what it has the potential to become.

> **You are the church. You are the body of Christ, perfectly arranged by God to carry out his mission for his world.**
> — 1 Corinthians 12:18

If your group is not healthy, the definition in the box to the right may not fit you today. Perhaps you are not seeing God's mission accomplished through your group at the present time. But I believe there is hope! I believe that God can transform your group into a robust and healthy expression of Christ's body.

In the pages to follow, I'll put on my doctor's scrubs and get out my diagnostic instruments to help you measure the health of your group. Then, I'll provide holistic cures to help your group become the healthy body that God designed it to be. If you are the group's leader, don't attempt to do this alone. Your whole group must be involved!

When "good enough" is not "good enough"

In *Good to Great,* Jim Collins opens with these words: "Good is the enemy of great. And that is one of the key reasons why we have so little that becomes great."[3] God promises to make us into something great (i.e. Genesis 12:2). Yet countless small groups settle for *good*. They acquiesce to ordinary and adequate rather than pursuing a transformational ministry.

GOOD SMALL GROUPS ARE THE GREATEST ENEMY
OF GREAT SMALL GROUPS

In *The Relational Way,* Scott Boren discusses the fact that we've settled for "a life of spiritual mediocrity and below-average small groups." In these groups, he writes, "people gather every week to help each other feel better about their lives, but there is no call to war, no call to enter into the spiritual battle to lead men and women from captivity. Instead, small groups become enclaves for what Eugene Peterson calls "the spirituality of narcissism."[4]

Small groups of believers generally do not form new groups with *below average* or even *good* as their goal. I think most want to accomplish something great for God. Somewhere along the way, they lose their focus and deteriorate. Their growth curve begins like this:

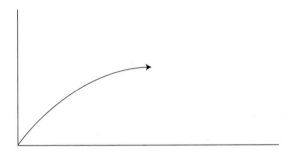

Through the years, I've learned that groups come to a number of decision points along their journey together where they will either (1) compromise for the comfy place of *good*, (2) fall into a death spiral and eventually be *gone,* or (3) get out of their comfort zones and pursue *great*. This is what it looks like in graphical form:

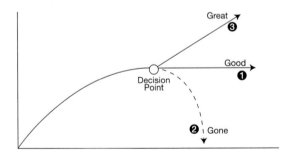

A *good* group can remain in this plateaued state for years, which is sad. They settle for nothing more, nothing less. They simply drift along in their lukewarm state without ever making much of a difference. Jesus says about such people, "I never knew you" (see Matthew 7:21-23) and "I spit you out of my mouth" (Revelation 3:16). I don't know about you, but I think we need to abandon any ideas of being forever good! If you stop and think about it, a group that is *declining* toward death (almost gone) should not continue to perpetuate this unhealthy position. Some groups just need to agree to disband and allow the members to reform in new groups that launch with more healthy values.

Are "good" groups healthy?

If good groups are ready to move from good to great at their next decision point, the answer is yes! To move from "good healthy" to "*great healthy*" (virile, vibrant, radically redemptive communities that make disciples, transform lives, and bear much fruit) they must be willing to make a change. Also it's very important to realize that many groups will need to *launch* at this basic stage of health, and then transition to a more dynamic group life later. If this concerns you or has you puzzled, don't worry. Each chapter of this book will describe how to make these vital transitions.

In *Good to Great in God's Eyes*, Chip Ingram writes, "great Christians don't play it safe."[5] The same is true for great small groups. They come to a decision point, and then resolve to do something risky or costly that requires great faith. Making that "no looking back" decision forces them out of their comfort zones and propels them toward greatness... even if they fail at first!

What fills the gap between good and great groups? Or, what do great groups do that good groups do not? The seven vital signs you will learn about in the rest of this book are found in this gap. Each vital sign provides specific actions you and your group can make at the decision points of your group's life to help you transform your group first to a good, healthy group and then to a great, overflowing group.

A GREAT, GOD-CENTERED MISSION

Missional is a very popular, trend-setting concept for some Christian writers and speakers. It's a powerful word that describes the focus of the church or small groups or even us as individuals. The way I like to define it is simply, "God's mission is our mission." While I will discuss this principle in several future chapters, I want to briefly introduce its vitality to all the rest of the vital signs here in the introduction.

Jesus gave his group a great collaborative mission and he gives the same mission to your small group: go and make disciples . . . teaching them to obey everything he has taught us. A great group is focused on God's mission rather than the group members' agendas.

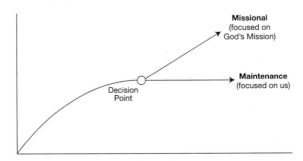

The fact is, many small groups in America are not missional. They are good at caring for one another and studying the Bible, which is good . . . but not great! Returning to *Good to Great*, Collins discusses our need to confront the brutal facts. In this book, I will help you and your small group honestly and diligently confront the brutal facts of your current reality in comparison to the truth of God's Word. This examination may lead you to a major decision point in your life together and move you off your comfy couches to do something God-sized . . . or remain where you are and maintain the status quo.

Our Church's Story

Status quo was not an option for us at Northeast Christian. In early 2009, I invested weeks of my time thinking and praying about how God wanted to move our groups to the next level so we could join him in that journey. Next, I consulted with other leaders and pastors I knew and read and re-read key resources, praying even more about what God wanted us to do. Finally, I adopted "The Seven Vital Signs of a Healthy Small Group." We developed and used an online assessment tool to survey our small group leaders on their perception of their groups' health.

After tallying all the results, we clearly understood how well or poorly our groups were doing in the seven vital areas, which gave us a point of origination for our journey. We used this information to coach our leaders, share insights when visiting groups, and developed ongoing training to shore up weak areas or gaps in our existing training. (By the way, I've included this assessment in Appendix E and it's also available online at http://www.touchusa.org/free-small-group-health-assessment.)

The health assessment data from our groups gave us energy, helping us see how we could help good groups become great over time. So for the next two years, we focused on the health of our small groups. We've learned that really good things happen when groups are healthy, which changed the way we strategically planned to grow the number of groups in our church. Instead of developing goals and plans based on starting X number of groups or leaders every quarter to connect hundreds of new participants in hastily formed groups, we have shifted our energy to deepening existing group health.[6] It's been a journey filled with ups and downs, but we're now seeing healthy groups grow and multiply on their own, making room for new members and new leaders.

Here's another benefit of focusing on the health of groups instead of numbers: When I first became involved in small group ministry, we told our groups they had to split or divide within a given time period (one or two years, for example). Many of our groups resisted and even revolted, so we got rid of the negative terms and began using more constructive words like *multiply* or *birth*. Changing the term did not make a difference because our people are intelligent enough to know how a forced "group divorce" feels regardless of the spin you put on it with a new term.

Through the years, I've done lots of vision casting, goal setting, and verbal arm-twisting to get groups to multiply. I've shown them Scriptures that clearly articulate the need to reproduce. I've illustrated the value of multiplying by sharing how in a healthy family the kids grow up and leave home to start a family of their own. I've handed out engraved relay-race batons to leaders who were charged with developing new leaders and passing their batons on to them. I've prodded, rewarded, celebrated, shamed, urged, and manipulated, but none of these tactics produced great results.

As we focus on health in groups through these vital signs instead of educational manipulation, our healthy groups naturally multiply without any pressure.[7] (I go into more detail about how this has happened throughout the book and especially in the conclusion, so keep reading if I've piqued your interest.)

In this book, I'll also share some remedies for what ails many small groups. I'm not promising these remedies will be pain-free or noninvasive. In fact, I will guarantee that if you take the health of your group(s) and your ministry seriously, it will involve some surgery. Focusing on group health instead of maintenance requires cutting out some unhealthy, perhaps even cancerous stuff.

To become successful, at each step you will need to ask yourself: *Am I willing to make the changes? Am I willing to take the chance? Is the payoff worth the risk of the investment?* Following Christ demands faith. Are you prepared to step out of the boat? Will you obey and follow God even if you're not sure where you are going? Do you have the faith to be compelled by the Holy Spirit (not me) to go somewhere new with your small group, not knowing what will happen to you when you get there? Are you ready for an adventure?

Then let's dive in!

THE SEVEN VITAL SIGNS

A healthy group is a *Christ-centered community.*
A healthy group has a *healthy, overflowing leader.*
A healthy group *shares leadership with a core team.*
A healthy group is *proactive.*
A healthy group lives in *authentic community.*
A healthy group *ministers to others.*
A healthy group is *a discipling environment.*

CHECK YOUR GROUP'S VITAL SIGNS NOW

To get the most out of this book, you should turn to page 184 now and complete the Healthy Small Group Evaluation for your group. After you've scored it, come back to this page. Complete the questionnaire below and then visit with your pastor or small group coach about your answers.

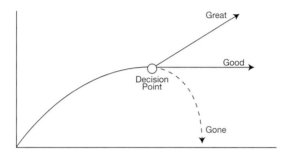

According to my assessment results, my group's current level of health is best characterized by one of the following statements:

❑ Our group was just formed. We are at a point of decision.

❑ Our group is currently doing great, God-sized things.

❑ Our group is a good small group; we clearly see the potential to be great . . . and I'm willing and ready to help our group achieve it.

❑ Our group is a good small group, and if we don't change anything, we'll continue to be a good group.

❑ Our group is effectively in a "death spiral" and will be gone sooner or later.

Regardless of which statement above best characterizes your group and your current energy level as a leader, *don't stop reading this book*. It is filled with information and practical help for leaders at all stages of maturity and experience. At the end of each chapter, you'll find a prescription page containing insightful questions to answer about the current health of your group. After reading the chapter, you'll know enough to fill in your own prescription for health for that vital sign.

VITAL SIGN #1:
A Healthy Group is a Christ-Centered Community

The most vital of the signs of a healthy small group relates to what is central to that group. This is the heartbeat; so let's pull out the stethoscope and begin with this fundamental principle:

> **Christ is central in a healthy small group, and a group cannot be genuinely healthy without Christ at the center.**

What I'm about to share might sound silly, but it illustrates my point. Healthy small groups are like Tootsie Pops®. The very best part is what's at its center! Twenty years ago when I was a new Christian, I read a little tract from Campus Crusade containing a diagram[1] that changed how I viewed my life. It contrasts two ways of living in this world, represented by two circles:

Self-Directed Life
Self is on the throne, directing decisions and actions (represented by the dots), often resulting in frustration. Jesus is outside the life.

Christ-Directed Life
Jesus is the life and on the throne. Self is yielding to Jesus. The person sees Jesus' influence and direction in their life.

Whatever you have placed at the center of these circles determines the kind of life you have. Only a Christ-centered and directed life results in a life overflowing with all the things God has for you. Because Christ is our power source, we can only accomplish great things with him at the center.

What if these circles represented your small group? Who's on the throne there? Is your group . . .

- Leader-centered?
- Challenge-centered (focused on a group member's or the group's issues)?
- Content-centered (focused on curriculum or a certain study or author)?
- Interest-centered (focused on an interest or affinity all members share)?
- Cause-centered?

Centering a group on one of the above will yield a good group, but a healthy (or *great*) group is focused on Christ's presence, power, and purposes.

Why do so many small groups fail to bear fruit? They have chosen to focus on a lot of things other than Christ. I've seen small groups take a lot of licks attempting to do group life centered on things other than Christ. So, here's the question: "How many licks will it take to get to the Christ-directed center of your small group?"

THE MOST VITAL HEALTHY-GROUP PRINCIPLE

Jesus provided the most vital principle for healthy groups and churches throughout his ministry. He modeled it and repeatedly taught it to his disciples. The principle is simple yet profound: God is not far away. When we keep our focus on him, he promises to be with us . . . leading us, moving us, working in and through us. He is our Companion. Jesus explained this principle most precisely in Matthew 18:20. He promised that whenever we gather together *in his name and for his sake* (because of him or for his purposes), he will be there among us.

When Jesus shared this, he was explaining the greatest of all kingdom principles for the time after he ascended: when his followers met together in his name, or because of him, or because they were his, he would be right there with them, through his Holy Spirit, in their very midst! He truly would never leave nor forsake them. He'd be with them—and us for that matter—to the very end of the age.

As you may have experienced or guessed, this does not happen automatically just because a small group of believers have gathered for a meeting in a home. It happens when the group members understand that the purpose and focus of the gathering is on Jesus Christ and his agenda for their time together and their lives.

I have discovered three barriers that keep individuals, groups, and churches from demonstrating this "depth of spiritual union" in Christ. Because these attitudes keep us from experiencing Christ's presence and power in our midst, they also block us from being healthy.

Barrier One: Consumerism vs. Christ-Following

Who or what is exalted in your small group? Only one person is worthy of being the ultimate focus of your group's attention, and, in a healthy group, it's not you, other group members, or anyone's needs in particular. In unhealthy groups, meetings revolve around individuals and people show up with their own personal agendas. They are consumers who believe the group exists to serve them. Christ-followers don't think this way. They put Christ in the center and exalt him above themselves (John 3:30).

Consumerism kills healthy community more than anything else, and it doesn't happen just because of "Extra-Grace-Required" people. In unhealthy groups, it can become the accepted norm where participants compete with one another for who can gain and keep the group's attention.

In a healthy group, there is certainly time for individuals to share their stories, what's happening in their lives, and their thoughts and feelings about various topics. But while doing this, they are purposely learning to *deflect the attention from themselves and aim the praise to Christ*. Good things like Bible study, serving, social times, prayer, and everything else on the agenda are all means to consistently expose and embrace Christ's purposes.

The first commandment is the foundation for this most-vital of the signs: "I am the Lord your God . . . You shall have no other gods before me."

God is supreme. He is our authority. If we don't get this one right as individuals, groups, churches, or society, we resign ourselves to a powerless, purposeless existence.

> **When Christ is not central to a small group, it's not a Christian small group. It's a person or cause-centered group.**

I know the statement to the left is strong, but it's true! Too many times I've seen good groups invaded by unhealthy, narcissistic, self-focused individuals who destroy the group. Here's a true story to illustrate this point, (with the person's name changed to protect her identity):

Susan skipped from one group to another in our church, poisoning each one. She crossed boundaries, insisted on her way, and bullied everyone she met . . . sometimes on her first visit! Susan's path of destruction included people who became fearful of small group involvement, deflated leaders, and closed groups. In one group, the leader and other group members didn't want to confront Susan because they were afraid of hurting her feelings, so they allowed her to take over and her needs became the focus. I intervened several times to bring balance to this group, and finally had to lovingly tell Susan she could no longer attend a small group until she got into counseling. Sadly, she left our church because she wasn't willing to acknowledge she had a problem.

Does all this sound hauntingly familiar? Leader, I implore you: do not allow this to happen! It is necessary to prayerfully act quickly. Your group should have no other gods before Christ!

Fortunately, I believe most groups are healthy Christ-centered communities that put Christ on the throne. They know that only his presence and power can transform lives, bring healing to hurting people, and make a permanent impact on others. And here's a wonderful by-product: These Christ-centered groups are naturally healthy in all the other vital signs. Why? Because *everything* else starts with Christ at the center!

Barrier Two: Focusing on the Historical Jesus but not the Incarnate Christ

Mark 6 contains a surprising story about Jesus returning to his hometown to teach. Verse 5 says, "Jesus wasn't able to do much of anything there—he laid hands on a few sick people and healed them, that's all" *(The Message). Huh? Did I read that right?* Jesus was not able to do much of anything?

Yes, in the midst of healing thousands, calming storms, raising the dead, and feeding thousands with a Lunchable®, Jesus experienced what human eyes would view as "failure." Was his power sufficient? Absolutely. It always is. But the people's stubbornness and unbelief was an obstacle to his effectiveness. The problem was not in Jesus' power; the problem was in man's heart. Jesus was simply too familiar to them. They knew of the Jesus from the past—still viewed as Joseph and Mary's boy—but they did not know the Jesus of Today . . . the Christ, the Son of God who has the power to bring healing and transformation to their lives.

Does this still happen? Have we become too familiar with the Jesus we grew up with to be healed and transformed by him? Do you know the Jesus of the past from Bible stories learned as a child, or do you know him and how he is working today in your midst?

When you meet as a small group, move beyond the stories of what Jesus *did.* Talk about—better yet, experience—what he is *currently doing.* He is indeed present in your group meetings right now!

Many small groups put an emphasis on studying, analyzing, and discussing the Jesus who appeared in the New Testament and walked the earth two thousand years ago. But they totally neglect the Christ who lives today in our midst. Friends, we need a far greater and timeless view of Christ![2]

Jesus is not far away, managing our efforts like a play director or, worse, a puppeteer. He lives in you and me and through his church. While he is physically seated at the Father's right hand, he is also with us through his Holy Spirit and is present with us whenever we meet together in his name and for his causes. What incredible power we have because of that!

A trend in many churches over the past several years involves gathering a group of unconnected church attendees in a circle. After a brief time of sharing, everyone is supposed to close their eyes, and on three, point to the person they think should be the leader of the group. If everyone in your small group sat in a circle, closed their eyes, and then simultaneously pointed to the *real* group leader, they should all point toward the center of the room, because your group's leader is Christ in your midst.

Barrier Three: Placing the Community Cart in Front of the Christ-Centered Horse

I love the images in Scripture of Jesus riding a horse into battle for us. Now imagine him riding a beautiful white horse, but the horse is pushing a cart full of people in your small group with its nose. This is not going to work, and yet, this is what we figuratively do in unhealthy small groups.

If you're like me, you believe in authentic Biblical community. You may even be passionate about it. After all, it has the power to transform lives, right? . . . *No it doesn't!* Only Christ can transform lives, and he uses community in that process.

Christ must be preeminent over our community for it to be healthy. Our relationship with him comes first. Community with one another flows out of our relationship with him. Finally, our ministry to the world flows out of our relationship with him and occurs in the midst of our Christ-centered community with one another.[3]

Henri Nouwen suggested that many Christian leaders start out in ministry by trying to do it under their own individual power. When that doesn't work, they beg others to help them. When human collaboration still isn't working, they decide to pray about it!

Jesus did the opposite. He began with God in solitude, then created a community who would carry out the mission together, and finally they served together. It was within that context of a "missional community" that Jesus made disciples.

Around my church, I'm known as the small groups champion or cheerleader. Several years ago, the leadership team at Northeast Christian Church came up with words that would describe each staff member's personality or passion. The word they used for me was *community.* That made sense, but to tell you the truth, I didn't like the label. Can you say pigeon-holed? Silo? Typecast?

We put the cart before the horse when we put community with one another before solitude with God. Nouwen said, "Why is it so important that solitude come before community? If we do not know we are the beloved sons and daughters of God, we're going to expect someone in the community to make us feel that way. They cannot."[4]

Perhaps some small groups are not very healthy and do not bear much lasting fruit because the group members invest so little of their time alone with God. Conversely, in a group where individuals have been alone with God, they arrive with hearts prepared to share out of an overflow which God has been privately revealing. They reach out to others from the overflow of what God is doing in their lives. They serve others together out of the overflow of one-on-one time with a loving God. And these same individuals step up to leadership because they sense God's calling upon their lives and submit to it, knowing it may be stretching but the faithful obedience is worth it.

Do you really want your small group to be healthy? *Start here!* Plan some solitary time with God. Then ask your group members what they are experiencing and hearing from God when they practice solitude.

HOW TO FOCUS ON CHRIST'S PRESENCE, POWER, AND PURPOSES IN YOUR SMALL GROUP

Practicing Christ's presence, living in his power, and existing for his purposes are high ideals. So how do we actually do these things as a small group?

Christ's Presence

Someone once said, "Never have a meeting to which you cannot invite Christ." What great advice! Here's how to do just that in your group:

1. Invite Christ into your daily life.

In the best, most healthy small groups, participants spend the week communing with God daily through time spent in his Word and in prayer, listening to him, and speaking to him. When the group officially convenes, members simply share what God has been doing in their lives the rest of the week. These groups don't have to be prodded to serve others or pray for people far from God. God has already placed his compassion in the hearts of the group members as he met with them individually each day.

2. Discuss Christ's presence when you gather.

Christ's presence with his people is a doctrine well-covered in Scripture. A few passages you could study together include Matthew 18:20; John 1:1-18 (v. 14 is the key); John 17 (especially v. 18); Zechariah 2:8-12; Daniel 3; and Revelation 21:1-7. Discuss how you can apply the principles in these passages to experiencing Christ's presence in your group meetings, as well as how different your gatherings might be if you experienced Christ's presence consistently.

3. Abandon the ordinary and comfortable to see Christ's presence.

Have you ever noticed how a brand new Christ-follower sees Jesus in more vibrant colors than most long-time church members? That's why I want to hang out with people who are seeking and finding a relationship with Christ. Their excitement for Christ is contagious! It's so easy for those of us who have spent years "going to church" and attending Bible studies to remain blind to Christ's presence. Remember the people of Jesus' hometown who knew about him, but did not really know him? Switch things up if this describes your group. Perhaps it's time for your group to move out of some of your normal group practices in order to see Christ Jesus anew. Here are a few ideas:

- Meet in your backyard, on a walk, or at a park, and take time to observe God's creation all around you. How do you notice his presence through his creation?

- Break the holy huddle. Bring new people, especially new Christ-followers and seekers, to the meeting. Allow them to ask the group tough questions. Engage with them in their search, and ask them how they currently see God working.
- Use a different method to study God's Word. Ask Christ to show you something new he wants you to see. (See Chapter 7 for more ideas.)

4. Practice listening to God's voice.

Jesus' followers know and listen to his voice (John 10:4, 27). He is the Good Shepherd and we, as his sheep, follow him because we know him. In the midst of all the noise of our world—voices calling us to follow this and that—Christ-followers seek to clearly hear, listen to, and follow Jesus' voice. Because the Holy Spirit has taken up residence inside of me, I can hear him speak to me internally, from my heart, not necessarily externally as an audible voice from heaven, like you see in the movies. Help your group members hear God's voice. When group members know the Shepherd's voice and are listening to him throughout the week, they will recognize his presence all the more when you all gather together. Urge them to practice solitude and ask God to speak in that still, small voice that Elijah described in 1 Kings 19:12.

5. Worship in creative ways.

Worship is more than singing songs in a church service or in your small group. When you learn to experience Christ's constant presence, worship is always in session! However, I think it's helpful to invest time during your gatherings to focus intently and purposefully on God. Nothing helps shift the focus of consumers more than turning their attention on Christ's presence, power, and purposes in your group. More than that, when a group worships God together, they are saying, in no uncertain terms, that God is the only one worthy to be exalted . . . not me, not my agenda, not the curriculum. Worship puts God in his rightful place as the real owner and leader of the group.

6. Pray as if Christ were in the room (because he is).

Almost all small groups pray, so why include this on the list of how to focus on Christ's presence? I don't know about your group, but most of the groups I've visited focus more on man and his concerns than Christ and his will during our prayer times. We spend twenty minutes or more sharing personal "prayer requests," which focus on our problems, our circumstances, and our friends and family members. Then, when everyone has shared, we pray all this back to God, as if he weren't present or listening to us. When we're done praying, or sometimes while we're still sharing our requests, group members often jump in with fixes for problems shared; recommendations of doctors, books, and web sites; or Scripture passages that come to mind as if these things were requested. This activity makes it very clear whose power the group members are most reliant upon. Man! Change your prayer time to focus more on God's concerns and to recognize that he really is present—and powerful—as you pray.[5]

7. Ask, "What is God up to here?"

Watch for how God is moving in your small group, and be ready to ask, "What do you think God is doing here?" or "What do you think God wants us to learn from this?" In other words, *as a group* learn how to see past the circumstances — what we normally see and hear —to see God's hands at work. Christ is not only present in your group . . . he is *powerful* too!

Christ's Power

Christ's presence activates his power in your group. Many people and groups seek God's supernatural power to do great things together. And they should, but they must *start* with Christ's personal presence with them. When Christ is *present* in a group, there is supernatural *power* available.

A healthy, Christ-centered small group can do all things through Christ who gives it strength. Why? Because Jesus has been given all authority in both heaven and on earth! Jesus' commission for his church in Matthew 28:16-20 reveals how his church is to operate. It begins with Christ's *presence*, as Jesus came to his disciples on the mountain. Next we see Christ's *power*, as he told them that he has all authority. Finally, we see Christ's *purpose*, as he gave them their mission.

The early church experienced this presence and power firsthand. In Acts 1:8, Jesus promised power when the Holy Spirit came upon his followers so that they could be his witnesses from Jerusalem to the whole world. That promise came true in Acts 2:4 when the apostles were filled with the Holy Spirit and began to boldly proclaim the truth. And it continued as these leaders remained true to their calling regardless of the circumstances: "[The religious leaders] brought in the two disciples and demanded, 'By what *power*, or in *whose name*, have you done this?'" (Acts 4:7, emphasis mine). Of course, Peter credited Jesus, the Messiah. While the religious leaders were astonished that these ordinary men were so bold, they noted that they had been with Jesus.

The early church knew where their power came from. They knew they could do nothing of any significance apart from Christ and his Spirit (John 15:5). This is why they were so committed to prayer. Prayer is, after all, the "power cord." If we don't pray, we're that very productive shop tool that remains dusty and unproductive until it's plugged into an electrical socket.

We can carry out God's work in two opposing ways, as illustrated below:

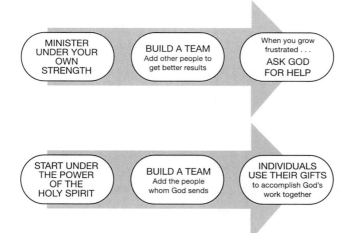

The kind of power that propelled the early church to transform their world is still available today to your small group, but it may require a radical mental shift. Here are just a few to get you started:

1. Realize it is not your group!

Mark 6 includes the account of Jesus feeding 5,000 people with five loaves of bread and two fish. I love Warren Wiersbe's illumination in his commentary: "The miracle took place in His hands, not in theirs; for whatever we give to Him, He can bless and multiply. We are not manufacturers; we are only distributors."[6]

Let me get personal for a moment: What are you holding dearly as your own today? Your small group? Your family? Your finances? Your ministry? Your career? When we place what we've been given into Jesus' hands—which is a deliberate act of surrender and stewardship—he has the power to multiply it. In his hands, he provides to overflowing (John 10:10). Of course, God does not work according to our whims and desires. Sometimes he multiplies his blessings in our lives in ways that we do not see at the time as blessings. As a popular worship song puts it, "What if the trials of this life are your mercy in disguise?"

Would you like to see your small group grow and multiply? Would you like him to bless your life? Place your group—and your very life—in Jesus' hands and then be a faithful steward in your role as one of his co-laborers.

2. Be prepared for God's power in your small group.

When you pray for someone, for example, pray with an *expectancy* of God's power to heal. As you plan to reach out to friends who do not know Christ, trust him to move mightily.

3. As a group, read the prayer of the believers in Acts 4:23-30.

These believers prayed with an expectancy of God to move through his power and according to his purposes. They understood the true power of prayer: "After they prayed, the place where they were meeting was shaken. And they were all filled with the Holy Spirit and spoke the word of God boldly" (Acts 4:31). Let their expectancy be your model as you pray as a group!

Christ's Purposes

When a group understands that Christ is present and powerful, they should naturally bend the knee to his purposes: his will, goals, and plans for the group.

I've found that as I lead a small group, I must constantly be called back to Christ's purposes and plans. It's very easy to get off track and start pursuing things that are not Christ's immediate purposes for our time together or the group at the moment. These may even sound like good things, but they are not where Christ desires for us to go at the moment.

In the chapters that follow, we'll talk about some of these good things, like authentic community, ministry, and discipleship, just to name a few. These are all solid group objectives, but when we pursue any of them for our own purposes or under our own power, we get off course from God's purposes.

How can you pursue God's purposes rather than your own? Here are four simple ideas:

1. Obey.

Committing yourselves to God's purposes and plans is an act of obedience. As God's children, he wants us to obey him, because his ways are always better for us than our own. Like disobedient children with free will, we can do our own thing our own way, but we'll suffer the consequences. Or we can choose to obey and be a part of God's purposes for his world. The good news is that God will even help us to obey him. "For God is working in you, giving you the desire to obey him and the power to do what pleases him" (Philippians 2:13, NLT).

2. Surrender your own expectations and perceptions of "success."

The context of Zechariah 4:6 is the rebuilding of the temple in Jerusalem. This temple was smaller than the original. As they built the foundation, it was obvious to observers that this temple would not be as impressive as the one built by Solomon. In verse 10, the Lord told Zechariah, "Do not despise these small beginnings, for the Lord rejoices to see the work begin, to see the plumb line in Zerubbabel's hand" (NLT). (Zerubbabel was the chief engineer for the project.)

Don't be anxious if your small group gets off to a slow start or isn't growing as fast as you expect. God rejoices to see new ministry begin when it's in partnership with him. He loves an entrepreneurial spirit! (God is,

While writing this part of this chapter, I began feeling rather depressed . . . as depressed as I can remember feeling. I steadily grew angry about some things going on in my life that seem out of my control. I knew intellectually what I needed to do, but I did not feel like doing it. I figured that this must be spiritual warfare, but truthfully, I was reaching for the white flag.

I came home from driving my son to school and sat down to read some e-mail. A couple of the messages were from small group leaders at our church, sharing things going on in their lives. Truthfully, I didn't feel like praying for them—I had my own problems—but I told them I'd pray for them anyway.

As I prayed, I felt a weight lift from my shoulders. I felt a little more sense of rest and peace. I know my circumstances have not changed, but something inside me changed: my focus. By praying for others, I took my attention off myself. Now, even as I write this, it is all still very fresh. I sense Satan still trying to push me back to worry, anxiety, and depression. So I did the only thing I know to do. I turned to my heavenly Father.

I prayed, "Father, I know I'm not supposed to be anxious about anything (Good Lord, I just wrote about this!), but the fact is, I am anxious about a lot of stuff in my life right now. I want to surrender these things to you. I know you've got this, but I guess I'm in the midst of this, and I don't see a way out unless . . . no, until you intervene. You are powerful. Help me once again to be still and know that you are God."

Then I did one more important thing. I called Chris, a guy in my small group, and asked him to pray for me. I'm home alone today, and needed to share what was going on and ask a good friend to pray for me, knowing he'll follow through.

after all, an entrepreneur.) Bigger is not always better. God rejoices in a job being done well and with integrity (which explains the significance of the plumb line in Zerubbabel's hand). Sometimes God *reduces* the numbers of participants to be more effective. If you don't believe me, read the story of Gideon and the Lord's army (Judges 7).

3. Commit to God's purposes together as a group and put it in writing.

I'll show you how to do this in Chapter 4 when I discuss the importance of goals and plans.

4. Partner with God. Remember, it is not by your own work or strength, but only by the working of God's Spirit that really matters.

God rejoices when we partner with him and do his work by the power of his Spirit. He accomplishes far more through this partnership than we could ever accomplish by our own power! And far more than we can even imagine.

Alone, your small group cannot change people's lives; that's Christ's job. He alone has the power to transform, but God has ordained us to participate. In other words, we are his hands and feet. When Christ is the head and heart of your small group, he will work through you in a divine-human partnership where participation is exciting. Talk often in your group about partnering with God—being his hands and feet!

A Christ-centered small group is the first vital sign of a healthy small group. It all starts here, but it definitely doesn't end here! While this first vital sign is the foundation of a healthy group—"The church's one foundation is Jesus Christ her Lord ..."—it's now time to start building strong walls. A healthy group cannot be built without them.

What will happen when you make Christ the center of your group? First, I think you'll find that the implementation of the rest of these vital signs will come much easier, because you'll have the power and direction you need. They will not come automatically, however. You still need to consider each one carefully and take the necessary steps to get healthy. Second, you'll find that your group will have purpose, and not just any purpose, but God's purpose. Third, and don't miss this, you as a leader can relax as you place the group in God's hands. For leaders, this makes all the difference—not only for the group's health, but for our mental and emotional health as well!

While Christ is the real leader of a healthy group, God has ordained to work through men and women after his own heart—leaders who know how to do just a few vital things so that God can work powerfully through them. What is a leader's role in developing a healthy group? That's the subject of the next chapter, in which I will speak to you about this vital subject leader-to-leader and from my heart to yours. A group cannot be healthy without a healthy leader!

CHRIST-CENTERED
CHECK-UP

Be sure to take the Healthy Small Group Evaluation on page 184 if you have not already done so. Then, use the following questions to help you analyze your results and come up with a treatment plan for your group. Discuss these questions with your core team (see Chapter 3) and then later with your whole group to build ownership.

1. How do you feel about your score on this most vital of all the vital signs? Does it seem to be a true indication of your health in this first area?

2. Look at the "Christ-Centered" questions for which you scored a 4 or 5. What specifically has your group done to be so healthy for each of those attributes?

3. Now look at the "Christ-Centered" questions for which you scored a 1 or 2. Why did you score low for this attribute? What obstacles are in the way to your group being healthy for that attribute?

4. Look back over the chapter and find principles that address your weakest areas in being a Christ-centered group. How can you *specifically* employ these principles in the next few meetings to become more Christ-centered?

5. To develop as a more Christ-centered group, the most important thing our group must to do is . . .

Pray about what you've written here with your pastor or coach.
He or she is eager to support you and help you and your group become or remain healthy.

VITAL SIGN #2
A Healthy Group has a Healthy, Overflowing Leader

My wife and I own a fifteen-year-old passenger van that still runs . . . and that's about the only positive thing we can say about it! It's dented, rusty, the windows and air conditioning don't work, it makes strange noises, and we are constantly repairing it.

When our nineteen-year-old son needed a vehicle, we gave him permission to drive it, but we told him it was his responsibility to take care of it. He drove it quite a bit, but didn't do much in the way of caring for it because it wasn't shiny and it didn't belong to him.

> **You are not the owner of your small group. It doesn't belong to you. The faster you recognize this, the healthier your group will become.**

Most of us do the same thing with the stuff in our lives we don't own. We forget we are *stewards* or *managers* of that which God has entrusted us. And at times, we even complain about what we have been so generously given.

Just as I own the title on our van, God owns the group you lead. The people in the group were his in the first place. Then he gave them to you to disciple and shepherd. Jesus modeled this perfectly. Jesus' prayer for his followers in John 17:6-12 was a prayer of stewardship: "They were yours; you gave them to me" (v. 6). I believe I'll one day be held accountable for what I do with those he puts under my care . . . some day, when the "Chief Shepherd" appears (see 1 Peter 5:2-4).

Your main job as a leader is to stay close to Jesus. Your leadership actually has little to do with you, your ideas, abilities, or even your gifts. It starts with what God is graciously pouring into you and then simply—but powerfully—overflows from your life into others God entrusts to you.

Godly leadership is one of my favorite subjects to write about. In three of my previous books, it's been a foundational principle, shared from what I learned at the time.[1] In this chapter, I will present some fundamentals about healthy leadership and share a few things I've been learning lately. If you want to pursue this topic deeper, I recommend one of my other books.

THE HEART OF SMALL GROUP LEADERSHIP

The first sign of a healthy small group is that it is Christ-centered. Rest assured that this will only happen when Christ is on the throne of your life or "*at home* in your heart" as the apostle Paul put it (Ephesians 3:17, NLT). This means Christ has taken up permanent residence in the very center of your life, including your will and emotions . . . in other words, all the things that make you *you*.

If Christ is not yet at home in your heart, I want to invite you to stop reading now and invite him in. If you are not sure what that means or how to do this, I suggest finding a Christ-follower who does and asking him or her to help you invite Christ into your life.[2]

If Christ is already in your heart, my prayer for you is that he will be more and more at home in your heart. May your relationship with him go way beyond a surface-level friendship to an ever-deepening communion with him!

Are you hospitable to Christ? Is he becoming ever-increasingly at home in your heart? Or do you treat him as a guest?

Think about that difference for a moment. What does it mean for someone to be at home in your house rather than just a visitor there? A resident has full access to everything in your home, free rein to go anywhere in the home without restraints. Does Christ have free rein in your life?

Overflow Leadership

Your life has a purpose. God has created and gifted you to do something you can do better than any other living person. You are a uniquely created vessel that God has been crafting through all those "random" circumstances of your life so far (see Isaiah 64:8). That vessel has been molded to do two main things: be filled up and overflow. Jesus told his followers that he came to give them life to the full, or "more abundantly" in some versions (John 10:10). The word *abundantly* means, "to overflowing." The vessel of your life is meant to be filled by God and then to overflow in ministry to the people he puts around you.

I explain this concept when I speak to leaders by using a cup and a pitcher of water. The pitcher represents God, who pours into us as we spend time with him, and the cup represents our lives, which overflow into the lives of the people he has put all around us as we spend time with them. One day after this session, a young leader came to the front and said excitedly, "I get it!" When I asked him what that meant, he explained that he had spent much of his time trying to lead by his own power rather than letting God simply overflow out of his life. He grabbed the cup I used as my prop and turned it upside-down in his hand, shaking it up and down like a big salt shaker: "I've kept myself busy attempting to minister by trying to sprinkle out onto others what I've put into my cup. But I've got the cup in the wrong position. I can't receive from God when I'm always running around trying to pour whatever's left in my cup into others." He took a breath and continued . . . "And most of the time I'm not really giving anything that's very good or helpful to people. I'm burning out because I have nothing left to give, and I'm not even bearing much fruit this way" (nodding to the downward-directed cup still in his hand).

Your primary job as a leader is to be filled up as you spend time with God. He will give you abundantly more than all you can ask or imagine! As I said in Vital Sign #1, solitude must come first for us as leaders, followed by being in community with others as a team, and then ministry, which flows out of the first two. Our model is Jesus, who "often ... withdrew to out-of-the-way places for prayer" (Luke 5:16, *The Message*).

Getting Out of the Way

Recently I spent a day at a local park. I was preparing to work on the following year's goals and plans for the ministry I lead and I wanted to hear from God. So I took a note pad and pen, bottled water, and sandwiches with me and ventured out to be alone with God.

Through years of trial and error, I've learned that if I want to hear from God, it's usually helpful to ask him specific questions and then to focus on listening. I've also discovered that God does not always answer immediately. I think that's because he wants to break me of my "drive-through" mentality for guidance from him.

At the park that day, I asked him specifically about what he wanted our goals and plans to look like for the following year, and then I waited . . . and waited . . . and waited! I walked some more and asked the question again, and waited some more. But I was not hearing anything. I think this is the point where many people give up, but I've learned to be patient. God will speak when and how he wants to speak, and I have no control over it, nor do I totally understand his reasons.

I asked the same question again (as if he didn't hear me the first time). I rephrased it (thinking he didn't understand me). I added more context to my question (thinking he needed more information). Finally I heard his response: *Maybe that's not what I want to talk about.*

"OK," I said out loud. "Then what would *you* like to talk about?"

Again, nothing.

At this point, I thought about how my wife and I take walks together. Sometimes we just need to get away from our four teenage kids and all the noise and distractions so we can talk without interruptions. I also considered the times when Heidi and I would walk at the park and neither of us would say a word. We just enjoyed being with one another and experiencing all the sights and sounds together.

As this thought was running through my head, that's when I sensed God speaking softly in my spirit: *Drop your agenda and plans for our time together Mike. What I really want out of today is for us to just spend some time together. Just be still . . . and know that I am God.*

This is difficult for many of us, especially in our fast-paced, always-connected world. Yet, what our Father wants is for us to just be still in his presence and know that he is God, that he is sovereign, and that everything is in his control. He's got a firm grasp on all my questions, anxieties about the future, and plans. My mind was flooded with words from Scripture: "Do not worry about tomorrow, for tomorrow will worry about itself" . . . "Do not be anxious about anything, but in everything, by prayer and petition, with thanksgiving, present your requests to God. And the peace of God, which transcends all understanding, will guard your hearts and your minds in Christ Jesus."

When I get alone with God and do my best to give him my undivided attention, he gives me—and I can't explain how—*his* undivided attention. And he takes great joy in this!

Later in the day, after spending time with God by walking through the woods and sitting next to a lake, God answered some of my

> **The Lord your God is with you,
> he is mighty to save.
> He will take great delight in you,
> he will quiet you with his love,
> he will rejoice over you with singing.**
> — Zephaniah 3:17

questions. He clearly showed me that my relationship with him was the priority. Then he gave me what I needed for the ministry.

Perhaps you're like me and you need more time in solitude in order to be a better, healthier leader. As the church today, we do a great job promoting community and ministry, but a poor job promoting solitude.

To get back to a place of solitude, you must prioritize your relationship with God by putting it on your calendar before other activities crowd it out. In this way you will "seek first his kingdom and his righteousness, and all these [other] things will be given to you as well" (Matthew 6:33).

Assumptions, Motives, and Expectations of Spending Time with God

One day I was reading and meditating on Habakkuk 3 when God spoke to me about three inner-life issues. Actually, he used this passage and the commentary I was reading to ask me three questions about my relationship and the time I spend with him. Perhaps this will help you as well:

> I trembled inside when I heard all this; my lips quivered with fear. My legs gave way beneath me, and I shook in terror. I will wait quietly for the coming day when disaster will strike the people who invade us. Even though the fig trees have no blossoms, and there are no grapes on the vine; even though the olive crop fails, and the fields lie empty and barren; even though the flocks die in the fields, and the cattle barns are empty, yet I will rejoice in the Lord! I will be joyful in the God of my salvation (Habakkuk 3:16-18, NLT).

1. What Are Your Assumptions?

Habakkuk's lips trembled with fear; he became weak-kneed and he shook in terror as he heard from God. In his commentary, Warren Wiersbe said, "Many people have the idea that it's always an enjoyable experience getting to know God in a deeper way, but that's not what the saints of God in the Bible would say."[3] That's true. Think about Moses who trembled in God's holy presence; Joshua and David who fell on their faces before the Lord; Peter, James, and John, who were left face down in terror at the Mount of Transfiguration; and John who fell at the feet of the glorified Christ in Revelation.

Do I assume that my time alone with God will always be nice and comfortable and peaceful, or am I ready for him to drive me to my knees as I come into his holy presence?

2. What Are Your Motives?

Wiersbe goes on to say, "God doesn't reveal Himself to superficial saints who are only looking for 'a new experience' they can brag about, or to curious Christians who want to 'sample' deeper fellowship with God but not at too great a price."

I had to ask myself some hard questions about this, allowing the Holy Spirit to honestly search me and know my heart, to test me and know my anxious thoughts, to see if there is any offensive way in me (Psalm 139:23-24). Are my motives pure when I come to him? Do I cherish my time alone with God because I might be able to write about it later? What questions would God ask *you* here? Do you study Scripture to look like a Bible scholar in your group? Do you have a quiet time so you can appear pious among your Christian friends?

All this begs a bigger question: Are our motives *ever* pure? I'm not sure. But I do believe God is calling me to make mine *more* pure. I need to test my motives as I go through my day. It's part of the practice of guarding my heart.

3. What Are Your Expectations?

One phrase in the Habakkuk passage really grabbed my attention: "I will wait quietly for the coming day when disaster will strike the people who invade us." Wow. When you study the book of Habakkuk, you see that this was not what Habakkuk wanted or had hoped for. This event would change everything and make life really difficult for God's people. But this phrase is more than Habakkuk's quiet resignation. It shows that Habakkuk trusted God completely and was totally surrendered to God's will.

Could I say, "I will wait quietly for the coming day when disaster will strike"? Could I have that kind of peace in the midst of chaos? Could I trust God, knowing my nice little life (a phrase borrowed from John Eldridge) was coming to an abrupt end? Habakkuk had a big disadvantage here. He was a prophet of God, so he knew what was soon to happen. Habakkuk did know what the future held, and he still trusted in the God who held the future in his hands.

Life to the full may not be what we've always thought it is. As Wiersbe says, "Habakkuk couldn't rejoice in his circumstances, but he could rejoice in his God!"

Leader, this is vital:
Do not spend time with God just to become a better leader.

Abandon all your assumptions, motives, expectations, and agendas for your time with him. Spend time with God because he is God. He is your Father who loves you deeply and yearns to spend time with you. He desires to fill you to overflowing with his love, mercy, wisdom, and power.

Your ministry is not your life. Your family is not your life. Your job, small group, church, hobbies, interests . . . are not your life. God is your life and he is the only one of these who can truly give life to you —real and eternal life, "more and better life than you can ever dream of" (John 10:10, *The Message*).

Guard Your Attitude

Your attitude as a leader is vital to the health of your small group. That's why your daily time with God is so important. It's the starting point for leading from the heart. Many leaders and groups fall into an "O, God . . ." attitude:

O, God, these people aren't really growing!
O God, why are they so uncommitted to the group?
O, God, why are we not serving more?
O, God, why don't we sense your presence?
O, God, why is this group not growing in numbers?

I've seen negativity like this frustrate and hinder a group's growth. Let me clarify. Yes, as leaders, we must take our concerns before God and surrender them to him. And yes, as shepherds we must be aware of and concerned for those entrusted to us. But don't allow yourself to turn negative! Instead, allow God to work in his own way and in his own timing, surrendering what you think and want. When you start thinking negatively and your emotions take over, you miss the "below the surface" spiritual growth that is happening. In many cases, one's spiritual growth is extremely difficult to measure.

If you or your group members find yourselves measuring the glass half empty all the time, try these three easy attitude adjusters:

1. Remember that your calling is to plant seeds, water, and cultivate. Let God do his part to bring the growth and fruit. This is important! Learn the difference between your role and God's and don't get the two confused!

2. Instead of "O, God," learn to say, "Yea God!" Celebrate what God is doing in and through your group and church. Remain ever-ready to encourage the baby steps you see in your group members.

3. When you pray together as a group, spend more time praising God and thanking him for what he is doing in your midst.

DEFINING SMALL GROUP LEADERSHIP

Why do small groups need healthy leaders? Throughout the Bible, whenever God was about to move, he started with *leaders*. Not hosts. Not DVD disc jockeys. Not facilitators.

Leadership is influence. Leaders are leaders because others are following. Maybe you've heard the classic John Maxwell maxim: "If you think you are a leader but no one is following you, you're just taking a walk!"

In his classic book, *Spiritual Leadership*, J. Oswald Sanders writes,

> The spiritual leader, however, influences others not by the power of his own personality alone but by that personality irradiated, inter-penetrated, and empowered by the Holy Spirit. Because he allows the Holy Spirit undisputed control of his life, the Spirit's power can flow unhindered through him to others.[4]

This brings me to my own definition of spiritual leadership, which shouldn't surprise you:

Leadership = Overflow

Yes, leadership equals influence, but your spiritual influence is only as great as what you have received from God through Christ. Paul wrote, "Follow my example as I follow the example of Christ" (1 Corinthians 11:1). This is a brilliant, one-sentence definition for Christ-centered leadership.

Leadership always envisions guiding people toward a specific goal. God led Moses to lead his people out of Egypt. He led Joshua to lead them into the Promised Land. He led Nehemiah to rebuild Jerusalem's walls. He led Peter and John and the other disciples to launch the church. He led Paul to take the gospel to the Gentiles.

To what or where is God calling you to lead your small group? This doesn't have to be a mystery. Jesus already provided the direction: "Go and make disciples." A Christ-centered leader leads people to follow Christ. You'll be told by lots of well-meaning people that your small group is supposed to do a lot of other things to attract members and keep existing members happy. But this is your main goal: *Follow Jesus*. After all, he is the real leader we are called to follow.

ATTRIBUTES OF HEALTHY SMALL GROUP LEADERS

One of the fundamental differences between good and great small groups is the spiritual vitality of the leaders. While imperfect, healthy leaders have a soft heart that God can use to accomplish his will. They are highly committed first to God, and *then* to the group. Jim Collins calls his initial good-to-great principle "Level 5 Leadership: a blend of extreme personal humility with an unwavering resolve for the company."[5] Healthy small group leaders also have a sense of personal humility and an ambition for God's kingdom. "Level 5" small group leaders have the following attributes:

1. Healthy small group leaders have been transformed

One of your high calls as a small group leader is to build an environment where spiritual transformation is experienced. This usually happens when the leader has first experienced transformation. The apostle Peter is a model of a transformed leader. Compare his attitudes and actions—and more importantly, his faith—between the gospels and Acts. Peter, like the rest of the apostles, was an unschooled, ordinary man whose life had been transformed by being with Jesus (Acts 4:13). Forty-three days before the events in Acts 4, he and his buddies were anything but bold—falling asleep on Jesus when asked to pray, running away from him in his hours of crisis, and denying they even knew him. They were still self-absorbed, worried, and protective of their lives.

Just forty-two days after Jesus' death, their faith was bold and courageous enough to stand up to the same religious leaders who were responsible for Jesus' crucifixion. What happened in between to bring about this transformation? It was a process that Jesus began three years earlier but that came to fruition with the power of the resurrection (John 20), the power of reconciliation (John 21), and finally the power of the Holy Spirit (Acts 2). Then Jesus used these transformed leaders to build a great, world-transforming church. He can do the same through you when you spend time with him and allow him to transform your life!

2. Healthy small group leaders live surrendered to God

One thing the apostles learned from Jesus was how to live and lead in surrender to God's will. Jesus instructed the apostles in Acts 1 to do one simple thing: wait. Their natural inclination would have been to jump into action, attempting to accomplish Jesus' vision under their own power. But they obeyed and waited in Jerusalem by praying and being patient for God to move. Once they received the promised Spirit, they carried out Jesus' mission in complete reliance upon and surrender to God (see 4:19-31 for one example) and in great power, I might add!

Great small group leaders turn to Christ for everything: who will be invited to join the group, the group's purpose, and the biblical content the group will apply during meetings. To do this, great group leaders pray and then wait before making decisions. This requires humility and self-control over one's emotional urge to act as quickly as possible. Great group leaders know if they surrender their leadership to Christ they will accomplish far more than they can do in their own power.

3. Healthy small group leaders are committed to their calling

God first calls people to lead, then he gifts them to lead, and last, he empowers them to lead.[6] I never twist people's arms to lead a small group at our church. But I do pray regularly for God to send us new leaders (see Matthew 9:36-38) and I often ask people if they sense God nudging them to lead a group. I believe God will send us the leaders he needs to lead groups at our church—and he does!

The leadership God has entrusted to you is a precious gift of grace (Ephesians 3:7) you should never take for granted. Accept it willingly, develop it, and multiply it by the mighty working of his power. Be a good steward of his gift to you!

4. Healthy small group leaders are friends

Jesus called his group members "friends." But perhaps that word meant more to Jesus than we think: "Greater love has no one than this," Jesus said, "that he lay down his life for his friends" (John 15:13). Real friendship is *sacrificial*.

A healthy group is comprised of genuine friends. A healthy leader considers the members of the group as his or her friends, not as students, participants, or "people who show up to our meetings." As the leader, you invest into those friendships. A group member from our church wrote:

> Joe and I have been in small group with Gary for about five years now. I wasn't sure about joining a "Bible study," but this group is so much more. The friendships we have formed are everlasting. Our small group, with Gary as our leader, not only studies the Bible, but we hold each other up; we encourage each other in good and bad times; we have moments where we laugh and sometimes cry; we love each other no matter what; and we know in our hearts that Jesus Christ is always with us. Gary keeps us focused, and he is one of the best friends Joe and I could ever have!

Wouldn't you want someone in your group to say the same about you? Become their friend!

5. Healthy small group leaders are friends with non-Christ-followers

Small group leaders may or may not have the spiritual gift of evangelism, but they do intentionally seek out friendships with those who are not yet friends with God. These friendships are genuine and unconditional . . . no strings attached. Yes, they pray diligently for their friends and watch for opportunities to share their story and the gospel, but they don't leverage the relationship to force conversations about Christ. Rather, they allow God to use them to shine his light. They allow the overflow of God's love to pour out of their lives naturally.

Jesus was known as a friend of tax collectors and sinners (Luke 7:34). Why? Because he "came to seek and to save what was lost" (Luke 19:10). Healthy leaders model this Christ-like attribute for the rest of the group. They model praying regularly for friends and neighbors who do not yet know Christ. They model inviting friends to the group. They team with other group members to pray for and reach out to seeking friends. They get out of their comfort zone to go into the world of non-Christians.

6. Healthy small group leaders are shepherds

Transformed, surrendered leaders invest relationally into and lovingly guide the group that God puts under their care. I believe being a shepherd is the main role of the small group leader. All the other attributes describe how to do this one well. Much has been written about shepherding in many small group books. I've written about it extensively in my other books, so I won't go into great depth here.[7] God's Word is rich in its discussion about shepherding. Here are just two passages that describe the shepherd-leader's role:

"He will feed his flock like a shepherd. He will carry the lambs in his arms, holding them close to his heart. He will gently lead the mother sheep with their young" (Isaiah 40:11, NLT). Great small group leaders invest relationally into the members of the group, and not just during group meetings!

"Be sure you know the condition of your flocks" (Proverbs 27:23). Do you know the spiritual condition of the people in your group? The biggest difference between a teacher, facilitator, or host and a shepherd-leader is that the former do not necessarily need to know their sheep or lead them spiritually. But that is precisely the role of the shepherd-leader.

As a small group shepherd-leader, you are in the most strategic position in the church to effect real, lasting life change and spiritual growth. But how?

- *As a shepherd-leader, be concerned for where people are in their spiritual journeys.* Treat each person with grace, not judgment. At the same time, help group members grow.
- *Personally assess where group members are on their spiritual journeys.* Spend time with them outside of meetings, asking what they believe, their spiritual practices, and their goals. Observe how they are living in relation to the fruit of the spirit.
- *Model a disciple's lifestyle.* You are a model for what life change looks like.
- *Keep providing the culture.* Continue to draw the group into increasing levels of authentic community. Don't give up meeting together, and people will be in a place where they can grow.
- *Provide a process for growth to happen.* This takes application-oriented Bible study as a group, one-on-one mentoring, serving together, and leadership development.

You are not the Chief Shepherd of the flock. That title belongs to Christ Jesus. Yet he has entrusted—as an act of stewardship—a small group of his people to you for this season. Therefore, "be shepherds of God's flock that is under your care" (1 Peter 5:2).

7. Healthy small group leaders are servants-first

Jesus made this one very clear. You can't be a leader in his kingdom unless you first have the heart of a servant. This is an attitude that comes through surrender to Christ as he transforms you into a humble servant.

Why do you want to lead? If it is because it is the best way for you to serve the group, then you are on the right track. If you desire leadership for any other reason, reconsider this role. Find another way to serve the group first.[8]

8. Healthy small group leaders are growing in competence

While leading a healthy small group has more to do with heart than skills, there are still some core competencies that will help you lead a healthy group. Others have produced long lists of competencies for small group leaders.[9] I won't reproduce them here, but do suggest you learn these competencies over time. On his blog, Ben Reed shared five skills good leaders usually have.[10] Here are his five and seven more of my own. Great small group leaders . . .

- Embrace the messiness of relationships
- Are quick to offer grace because they've been given so much [grace]
- Ask for help
- Look a lot like good pastors
- Are patient with group members who are difficult to love
- Pray regularly for group members
- Encourage
- Keep the group moving toward goals
- Practice authenticity/transparency
- Are quick to listen and slow to speak
- Ask great questions
- Lead as part of a team

Now here's the good news: you don't have to do all of these alone! In fact, healthy leaders share group roles with a Core Team and the rest of the group. I'll talk more about that subject in the next chapter. Just don't forget: God did not make a mistake when he called you to be the shepherd-leader of the group he's put under your care. When you are healthy and growing spiritually, your group will also be healthy and growing. That's

God's plan. So I encourage you to commit right now to this vital principle. Your group will not be healthy without you as a healthy leader!

And when the Chief Shepherd returns and you come face to face with him, his words to you will be: "Well done, good and faithful servant!"

THE OVERFLOWING LEADER'S CHECK-UP

1. As a leader or core team member, how do you feel about your overall score on this vital sign? Does the score feel like an accurate indication of your health as a leader?

2. Look at the questions for which you scored a 4 or 5. What specifically have you done to be healthy in each of those attributes?

3. Now look at the questions for which you scored a 1 or 2. Why did you score low for this attribute? What obstacles are in the way to you as a leader being healthy for that attribute?

4. Look back over the chapter and find principles that address your weakest areas in being a healthy leader and note them below. Then ask yourself, "How can I employ these principles to become a more Christ-centered leader?" and write out your responses. (Not a simple task, but worth it!)

5. Finish this statement: To develop as a healthier leader, the most important thing I need to do is . . .

Pray about what you've written here with your pastor or coach.
He or she is eager to support you and help you and your group become or remain healthy.

VITAL SIGN #3
A Healthy Group Shares Leadership with a Core Team

One night during a small group meeting, Chris said he thought we should bring all the kids into the living room and, as parents, pray with and for them. After the kids came in, sitting on their parents' laps and on the floor in front of us, Chris glanced over at me. I just nodded at him, and he started leading the prayer time. Adults and kids prayed and worshiped God. Several of the dads prayed prayers of blessing upon the children. What an awesome time of prayer!

Chris is one of our group's core team members. Years ago, when I used to lead alone, that special time of prayer would not have happened. Why? I didn't have a team. But Chris and others are now empowered to lead, and our group experience is far more powerful. One of the biggest secrets to leading a healthy, vibrant, life-changing small group is sharing leadership with a core team.

> **A healthy small group is team-led by two to four members who share the role.**
>
> **No one leads alone.**

[In *The Pocket Guide to Burnout-Free Small Group Leadership,* I detail how to find and utilize a core team. I will summarize some of the main points of that book in this chapter and share new things I've learned since it was released.]

CONCENTRATE YOUR DISCIPLE MAKING EFFORTS

How many people can you effectively lead, shepherd, and disciple? Let me ask the question another way: If you are to bear much fruit, fruit that will last . . . if you are to see true transformation of people's lives . . .

if you are to see people develop into leaders so that you multiply your leadership . . . into how many people can you invest your life?

Jesus formed a small team that would eventually change the world. But first he called two sets of brothers. Three of those four, Peter, James, and John, became Jesus' inner circle or what could be called his core team. Jesus poured his life into these three men, investing into them and modeling a life surrendered to the Father. He took these three away with him to pray and heal, as well as when he was transfigured.[1] While Jesus did not ignore the other nine apostles or his other followers, he concentrated his time on these three to develop them into leaders.

Jesus knew something vital that we may overlook: No one can effectively lead, disciple, or shepherd more than about three people. Even Jesus didn't attempt it. Leading, discipling, and shepherding are based on close relationships in which the leader invests into the lives of those he or she is leading.

Small Groups Are Too Big!

Disciples are not produced by programs, events, or even "discipleship studies." They are made in the context of authentic community by individuals through the power of the Holy Spirit. Disciples are made life on life. Leroy Eims wrote, "It takes individual, personal attention. It takes hours of prayer for them. It takes patience and understanding to teach them how to get into the Word of God for themselves, how to feed and nourish their souls, and by the power of the Holy Spirit how to apply the Word to their lives. And it takes being an example to them of all of the above."[2] Small groups cannot accomplish this. And leaders cannot achieve this on their own with a group of eight to twelve.

Discipleship is a personal relationship in which one believer pours his or her life into another to help that person become more like Jesus. I think most people can make this kind of investment with at most two or three people at once. In the best circumstances, these two or three should be people within your small group.

The small group as a whole is where you do life together, serve together in missional community, and discuss and apply the Bible together. It's also a warm and welcoming place where you can invite friends who do not yet know Christ, where they can see the love portrayed in your community life and meet the One who makes it happen.

This table summarizes some of the intentional differences between the larger small group and the subgroup of two or three.

Small Group	Two or Three
Social belonging: a group of friends, perhaps very good friends	Personal belonging with trusted friends
Do life together	Gather regularly for intentional discipleship
Discuss and apply the Bible together	More intense study of God's Word, memorization, personal application, and accountability
Worship and pray together	More personal prayer and confession
Serve together	Specific discusson and accountability for how we are serving and sharing our faith
Invite others in; pray for one another's lost friends	

Group members often balk when faced with the proposition of deeper prayer, accountability, and especially confession in the group. And for good reason! Most small groups are too big for these biblical practices. But a core group of two or three is just right.

I want to be clear that I'm not advocating a new program or system for small groups consisting of no more than four people. I'm simply pointing out that there are limits as to how many people you can effectively lead, shepherd, and disciple. And I believe that number is two or three.

Core Teams and Apprenticeship

Core team members are much more than leaders-in-training, apprentices, or interns. They are not just in training to eventually become future leaders, they share leadership together. Leadership development comes more naturally and organically in the core team. However, from personal experience I've learned that a form of apprenticeship still works within the core team. The one-on-one relationship between the leader and an apprentice goes even deeper and is even more intentional than with the rest of the core team. Jesus' intentional leadership development (apprenticeship) of Peter is a perfect example. Out of your core team, you may have one person whom God has given you to be the next leader. All core team members are potential leaders; in fact, everyone in the group is a potential leader. But one person may be the *next* new leader. You will focus your time with him or her, but not exclusively. You will need to find a balance here. Don't neglect the rest of the core team. Share leadership with all of them according to their gifts. Call out their passion and envision them with God's calling on their lives. Love each of them and invest into each of them individually and as a team.

In his book, *Natural Church Development,* Christian Schwarz reports, "The planned multiplication of small groups is made possible through the continual development of leaders as a by-product of the normal group life."[4] Note the last part of this sentence. Leader development is a "by-product" of normal, healthy, holistic group life. It is not forced. From my own observation, sometimes it even comes as a surprise, even though it was a value from the beginning.

I intentionally invested into Chris, the core team member who led the prayer time I discussed in the beginning of this chapter. I met with him regularly for lunch to talk about our group and make plans together. He led parts of the meeting and I provided feedback when we met. Other core team members were also involved in leading, but I was even more intentional with Chris. Eventually, my wife and I left the group in Chris' hands so we could join with another new leader to launch another group. Chris already established a core team and was doing a lot of the leading, so the transition was easy. The group grew immediately.

DEVELOP LEADERS WITH A CORE TEAM

I'll talk more about discipleship later in the book, but I need to define it here as it relates to working with a core team. Today Christians accurately define *disciple* as a follower of Christ who is maturing. But Jesus and others used the word to describe something more. When Jesus called his core team members, he told them he would make them into fishers of men. Over the next three years he taught them about and modeled servant leadership for them. These leaders then did the unthinkable. God used these unschooled ordinary men to change the world.

I've known highly skilled and gifted leaders who were not able to develop new leaders. When I've asked them why, they have admitted that while they were talented in some aspects of leadership, they were *not* good at sharing leadership. They did it all themselves because they had the abilities to do so. But this leadership style did not bear fruit or a legacy of leaders.

Dr. Bill Donahue provides seven common reasons why leaders don't share leadership.[5] Do any of these describe you? (I've added explanations after each one.)

Loss of control: Whenever you give something away, you lose some control. There is a risk involved in sharing leadership. It takes trust. Weigh the risks versus the rewards of trusting others more.

Feelings of inferiority: A leader with a low self-esteem may worry that the core team members may become better leaders than themselves. As Donahue says, this is actually called "success"!

Self-centeredness: To lead a core team, you must have genuine humility. This does not mean you are passive or weak, however. Team leaders "don't think less of themselves, they just think of themselves less."[6]

Feelings of inadequacy: Some leaders don't believe they have much to offer to their core teams. Remember, you were called as a leader not because of what you know, but *Who* you know.

Fear of failure: You might fear picking the wrong people for your core team or that you'll somehow fail at developing them as potential leaders. Again, your job is to team with God in planting seeds and cultivating them. God makes things grow.

Short-sightedness: I believe this is the biggest reason so many good leaders fail, so I'll spend a little more time here. Quite often, leaders can't see the potential for leadership in other group members. Even though the leader has exceptional facilitation skills and Bible knowledge, the group struggles. Group members do not sense they are really needed, so they are not as committed to the group as they could be. If this describes you and your group, admit the issue and swallow your pride. Other group members may not lead the same as you or as well as you do, but that's OK. If you find you are a perfectionist, work at becoming flawless at sharing leadership even if others are not as good as you!

False Perceptions: Faulty thinking and assumptions can keep a leader from sharing leadership. Some leaders never learned to share leadership, so they think they are supposed to do everything . . . and they do. Another false idea is "no one wants to help me lead." In reality, most Christ-followers are looking for more opportunities to use their gifts and serve others.

The beauty of shared leadership is that the individual burdens are lighter. Apologize to the group for not asking sooner. Show group members that you believe in them and encourage them to share leadership using the gifts God has given them.

If anyone in the group says they feel unworthy to lead, tell them not to say that about God. After they get over the initial shock of that statement, tell them that they are a treasured child of the most high God and that he has gifted them to have an important role in his kingdom.

Kevin and Jamie Clark are a couple in our church whose groups have multiplied several times. They simply invest into and share leadership with other couples in their group, and then wait for God to move. After some time passes, they leave the group in the hands of one or more of these couples and launch another new group. They remind me of the apostle Paul who often started churches and then left disciples like Timothy or Titus behind to strengthen those communities, as Paul moved on to another city to plant another church.

What's the difference between the Clarks and other leaders? They share leadership and have a strategy and steps for discipling and developing members corroboratively.

HOW TO DEVELOP A CORE TEAM

So how do you move from leading solo to team-leading the group? Here are nine steps you can take to make this a smooth transition.

1. Move over. Practice Christ-centered stewardship of the group by moving to "second-chair" leadership. This is an act of surrender on your part.

2. Share the load. Ask God to show you whom you should ask to be part of the core team and begin to share leadership with them. Some leaders find asking two or three members out of the group to be tricky. Either they don't think anyone will say yes or they are afraid people's feelings may be hurt by not being asked.[7] Here are a few things that will help you discover the right people for the team:

- *Don't recruit,* at least not in the usual way we usually think of "recruiting." Instead, ask the Lord of the Harvest to send these "workers." Trust him to help you know who to ask.
- *Know what you're looking for.* Look for potential, not perfection. Look for servants, not saints. Look for humble hearts, not superior skills or incredible intelligence.
- *Look around you.* Perhaps God has already put your core team members right around you. They may be the people in the group with whom you already have close relationships or those whose gifts complement yours.
- *Don't do it all.* People hesitate to be on a team when the leader does too much. As the group's steward leader you must grow in your ability to allow others to use their gifts.

[Some leaders have the auspicious problem of having too many members who think they should be on the core team. If this describes your problem, be sure to read *The Pocket Guide to Burnout-Free Small Group Leadership*, which explains how to handle this situation.]

3. *Don't go back!* I've known leaders who have a core team but then continue leading alone. Don't do it. In fact, ask your core team to hold you accountable. The next step will help with this.

4. *Create a clear plan of action.* Who on the core team will do what and when? How will you communicate with one another? How often do you want to meet separately from the group to play, pray, and plan? Ask everyone on the core team to write down the decisions made when you meet.

5. *Become a team.* Enjoy fun activities together and build friendships with one another as a core team, away from the other members of your group. Take a ropes course or go camping together. Eat together. Love one another. Bond with them and let them bond with you.

6. *Share roles.* Share the shepherding of the group. Look at your group's roster when you meet with your core team. With whom do your core team members have natural relationships? Utilize those friendships as a point of origination to shepherd them through the core team members. In one group at our church, a core couple with young children strategically shepherded the other couples with kids. It was a natural alignment. Later, as the group grew, the couples with kids launched a new group. It could not have happened more organically and easily!

7. *Actively develop core team members.* Leadership development is easier with the core team approach, but it requires intentionality on your part. For example, strategically give your core team members opportunities to lead group meetings. Then visit with the core team to encourage

and provide feedback. If you do this with other core team members, everyone will benefit and become an encourager. I like doing these recap sessions right after a meeting, when possible. They don't have to be long meetings, but they sure are powerful for developing core team members into future core team leaders.

8. *Attend training sessions together.* When your church has leadership training, recognition, or other small group leadership events, the whole core team should attend. If your church only invites the main leaders to these trainings, extend an invitation to your core team. (Of course, make sure you've received approval from your church ministry leader first.)

9. *Extend the Kingdom.* Core teams make for healthier small groups, and healthy small groups grow. As you move to a core team approach, your group will surely grow and multiply. It is just the natural result of doing small group leadership as a team. In my church, we do not put any time limits or size limits on groups. We simply help them become healthy and the groups branch off or multiply naturally.

Valerie is a core team member in a woman's group. About a year ago she told me she thought she was ready to start her own group, so we discussed a time line. She came to our training class. She's helped lead. Then life grew hectic. Her brother was in a car accident and was in a coma for weeks. When he came out of it, Valerie became one of his primary care-givers. Leading a new group would have to wait. Through all of this, I believe God has been preparing Valerie for leadership. She has grown in her relationship with God, trusting and depending on him more than ever.

I never asked Valerie to step up and lead. But her leaders and I have continued to invest into her and allow God to overflow from our lives into hers. Valerie would not say that I or her small group leaders have called her to leadership; she'd say God has called her. I can't wait to see what he will do through her as a leader!

> **A Christ-centered group . . .**
> **with a Christ-centered leader . . .**
> **who shares leadership with a few others . . .**
> **creates a healthy small group!**

These are the first three vital signs that make groups flourish. Your job as a leader is to start with these three principles. When you team with God and your core team, you will see God's Kingdom extended to more and more people. You really will make more disciples by focusing on less, just as Jesus did. You can do this, whether you are launching a new group with a core team or beginning to share leadership in your current group.

Sharing leadership will keep you from burning out as a leader. Just as importantly, it is far more fun and rewarding than leading alone!

THE SHARED LEADERSHIP'S CHECK-UP

1. What does your score on this vital sign tell you about how you are sharing leadership with a core team?

2. Look at the questions for which you scored a 4 or 5. How specifically has the sharing of leadership helped your group to be healthier?

3. Now look at the questions for which you scored a 1 or 2. Why did you score low for this attribute? What obstacles are in the way to your group being healthy for that attribute?

4. Look back over the chapter and find principles that address your weakest areas in sharing leadership with a core team. How can you employ these principles to do a better job of sharing leadership?

5. Finish this statement: To become healthier as a group by sharing leadership as with a core team, the most important thing I or our group needs to do is . . .

Pray about what you've written here with your pastor or coach.
He or she is eager to support you and help you and your group become or remain healthy.

VITAL SIGN #4
A Healthy Group has Proactive Leadership

"A failure to plan is a plan for failure." *- Benjamin Franklin*

One day I decided I needed to clean out the gutters on the dormers of our house. But our roof has a very steep pitch and these gutters can't be reached using a ladder set on the ground. I needed a way to get up the steep roof to the gutters. I figured that if I could tie something to the back deck and throw it over the house, I could scale up the roof to the dormers. But I didn't have a rope long enough. I looked around, and the longest thing I had was a garden hose.

> **A healthy small group is proactive, not reactive.**
>
> **It lives by design.**

I tied the hose securely to a 4x4 post on the deck and, after several tries, threw the hose over the top of the roof. I climbed the ladder, got a good grip on the garden hose, and started climbing. Here's what I didn't plan for: garden hoses stretch! In fact, when you put 175 pounds of force on a 100-foot strand of standard-grade hose, it stretches *really* fast. I found myself dangling in front of our house, with just enough hose to get back to the ladder and to the ground without falling or losing too much of my pride.

So I went directly to "Plan B." I called a friend who cleans chimneys and has the correct equipment to climb around on roofs.

I didn't have a very well-thought-out plan, and the consequences could have been disastrous. I get into trouble like this quite often, "flying by the seat of my pants." We can be like that with our small groups, too, just making it up as we go along in a reactive way. We may even claim this is more spiritual (dependent on the Holy Spirit). But the Holy Spirit will be involved in wise planning as well.

Bill Willits, Director of Group Life at North Point Community Church, tells the story of when that church first began meeting in the convention center in Atlanta.[1] The electronic marquee that thousands of people would see everyday advertised the church as "No Point Church." The sign engineer could not fit the entire name on the marquee, so he took some creative liberties. Of course, Willits says, this became the joke of the night, but it also provided Pastor Andy Stanley an opportunity to remind the new church of their need to stay focused on what God had called them to do.

What's the point of your small group? What's your mission? What are your goals? The point of this chapter is to help you think through these questions.

You can live either by default or design; in reactive mode or proactive mode. Most people live most of their lives by default. In other words, life happens to them. The same is true in many small groups. However, having written goals and plans is the difference between default and design, and, often, between unhealthy and healthy. When a group is struggling, when they are not bearing much if any fruit, that's probably a sign that the group is in reactive mode.

Look Down the Trail

I have learned a lot about being proactive rather than reactive on my mountain bike. An important skill in mountain biking is to look down the trail, past what's right in front of you. When you look five to twenty-five feet down the trail (depending on the type of trail), you can identify potential hazards and challenges before you reach them and create a plan of action. Take it from me, constantly looking just ahead of your front tire results in a jerky, stumbling ride and some painful blunders.

In mountain biking and in leading a small group (or anything, for that matter), you want to make decisions *before* you actually get there (wherever "there" is at the time). Know where you are going, not just where you are at this moment. I've witnessed many groups in reactive mode. Their longest range plan is what they are going to do next week. (Some groups don't even plan that far ahead!)

When I'm mountain biking and I start thinking I might crash, guess what often happens? Yup . . . I crash! But when I am looking down the trail with positive expectations, the ride flows and is fun. In a healthy group, the members take time early and often to look down the trail. They are prepared and they don't freak out at little challenges along the way. They grow, reach out, serve, and develop new leaders. They excitedly look ahead to "what's next?" This is what you want in your group!

Jesus' Goals and Plans

As Jesus called his followers, he told them, "Come, follow me and I will make you fishers of men." This little statement contains both his goal and his three-year plan for them:

GOAL = for them to become fishers of men

PLAN (method for accomplishing the goal) = to follow him

The early church in the Book of Acts also had goals and plans, which Jesus gave them: "You will receive power when the Holy Spirit comes on you; and you will be my witnesses in Jerusalem, and in all Judea and Samaria, and to the ends of the earth" (Acts 1:8).

GOAL = for the gospel to reach Jerusalem, Judea, Samaria, and eventually the whole earth

PLAN = to be his witnesses as empowered by his Spirit

Jesus lived a proactive life according to his Father's design. He lived each day with the goal in mind he was sent to accomplish. He lived according to the plans of his Father. Toward the beginning of his earthly ministry he said, "For the very work that the Father has given me to finish and which I am doing testifies that the Father has sent me" (John 5:36). At the end of his earthly ministry he prayed, "I have brought you glory on earth by completing the work you gave me to do" (John 17:4). Then he gave those same goals and plans to his closest followers when he prayed, "As you sent me into the world, I have sent them into the world."

Jesus warned those who wanted to follow him to carefully consider the costs. He told them to look down the trail first to be sure they were making the right choice (See Luke 14:28-33). Jesus encouraged those who wanted to follow him to live proactively. He illustrated how foolish it would be to go into something without wise planning—like laying a foundation without being able to finish the job or going to war without considering if you have the troops to win . . . or climbing your roof using a garden hose!

WHOSE GOALS AND PLANS?

Some people believe it is wrong for a Christian, a church, or a small group to set goals and make plans. In their book, *A God-Centered Church,* Henry and Melvin Blackaby say that setting goals "comes straight from the world and the culture around us." The authors go on to say, "As servants of the most high God, we don't have the right to determine the direction of our lives or our church. God alone sets the purposes, objectives, and goals for His people."[2]

So am I off base in writing this chapter to encourage you to set goals and make plans? I don't think so. I see plenty of Biblical support:

- "May [God] grant your heart's desire and fulfill all your plans" (Psalm 20:4).
- "Wise planning will watch over you. Understanding will keep you safe" (Proverbs 2:11).
- "Good planning and hard work lead to prosperity, but hasty shortcuts lead to poverty" (Proverbs 21:5).
- "I press on toward the goal to win the prize for which God has called me heavenward in Christ Jesus" (Philippians 3:14).

The issue is not whether we should set goals or make plans; the issue is *whose* goals and plans!

- "The Lord foils the plans of the nations; he thwarts the purposes of the peoples. But the plans of the Lord stand firm forever, the purposes of his heart through all generations" (Psalm 33:10, 11, NLT).
- "Commit to the Lord whatever you do, and your plans will succeed" (Proverbs 16:3).
- "Many are the plans in a man's heart, but it is the Lord's purpose that prevails" (Proverbs 19:21).
- "Are you so foolish? After beginning with the Spirit, are you now trying to attain your goal by human effort?" (Galatians 3:3).

No, we don't have the right to make our own *man-centered* plans or try to accomplish our goals by human effort. God will not fuel or empower those kinds of plans and goals. But when we commit to following *his* plans and purposes, they will succeed, prevail, and stand firm forever!

As you discuss goals and plans as a group, ask these questions:

- What is God doing, and how can our small group join him?
- What adjustments do we need to make in our group in order to fulfill God's purposes for us?
- What does God want to accomplish in and through our small group this year?
- What has he been saying to us as a group that we must carefully obey?

The Spirit's Perfect Timetable

Right after Heidi and I got married, we moved into a large apartment building. We wanted to start a small group to reach the unbelievers who lived there, but we had no idea how to get started. So I asked Glen—a minister at the church we attended—how we should proceed.

"I don't think you should start a group yet," he said.

His response surprised me. "But it's a perfect opportunity," I told him. "We think we can make an impact on the people there through a small group."

"That's great," Glen replied. "But first, you should build some friendships, pray for the people there, and then ask some of those friends to a small group when the time is right."

So I asked, "But how will we know when the time is right?"

"Just pray," he said. "The Holy Spirit will let you know."

That wasn't the answer I was looking for. My pragmatic nature wanted a ten-point implementation strategy. But we did what Glen suggested by making friends, praying, and watching for the Spirit to move. We found out where people liked to hang out, and we hung out with them. We looked for opportunities to build friendships as we rode the elevator, did laundry, and helped people who were moving into the building. We went to parties and game nights in the apartments around us. We drank our cokes while they drank their beers—and we discovered our sobriety helped us win the games as the night progressed! We asked them about their lives and family, listened to them, loved them, and did not judge them. But we lived as Christ-followers before them. Most importantly, we prayed, seeking God's green light. We waited and watched for the Spirit to move.

A year and a half later we were still praying and watching. I was thinking Glen was crazy. We wondered if the Holy Spirit would ever "let us know." Then one evening Sherry, the apartment building manager, stopped me. She told me that Sigma, who lived in the building with her boyfriend, Vic, had been approached by a member of a cult and invited to attend a Bible study with them. Sherry asked me to talk to Sigma about this cult.

Sigma and about six other people from our building were sitting around a table by the swimming pool. I told Sigma what I knew and answered her questions. Suddenly, a long haired guy named Marty, who had a reputation for being a pothead, interrupted me. "Wait a minute," he said. "Sigma's been invited to a Bible study by this group, right?"

"Yeah, that's right," I confirmed.

"Well, is there anything wrong with her going to a Bible study?" Marty asked.

"No, not at all," I explained. "It's just that . . ."

Marty jumped in again: "So why don't we just start our own Bible study here?"

Someone else quickly chimed in, "Yeah, we could meet at different people's apartments each week. We could invite other people from the building too!" Others jumped in and suggested rotating apartments, who would provide food, and how often they would meet.

Then Sherry looked at me and said, "This sounds great, but we need someone who knows the Bible to lead this. . . . Mike, you're the only one here who knows anything about the Bible. Would you lead it?"

I don't know . . . I'm still waiting for the Holy Spirit to let me know. The thought only went through my mind for a split-second until I realized it was the Spirit moving!

I agreed to lead it and then sat back in my chair and let them plan the whole thing. A week later, we started a small group focused on the basics of Christianity. Vic came to Christ the second week. I baptized him in the apartment building's swimming pool early one Sunday morning, waking up half the building when Vic let out a whoop as he entered the cold water. Sigma gave her life to Christ about a year later. Eventually everyone in that group turned their lives over to Jesus, some after we had moved away from the building.

My initial plans were in line with God's purposes. But they were still *my* plans, my timing, my initiative, my work. I had made myself the main character in the story. When I followed Glen's advice, however, God's purpose prevailed. Let me reiterate here that following God does not equal being inactive. Heidi and I actively followed God as he led us into relationships before we started the small group.

One Degree of Separation

Making your own plans may not initially seem like a big deal. I can just hear a group leader think, *We won't get that far away from God's will by making one small decision ourselves, right?* It's true: when you go your own way, you may not even notice it at first. It's just one degree of separation from Christ's purpose. (Check out the diagram on the top of the next page and you'll see what I mean.)

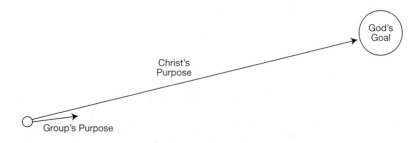

But over time, that path will take you further and further away from God's will.

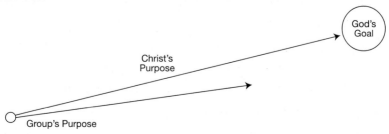

As if this isn't bad enough, the group will come to other decision points along the way. When you choose your own purposes rather than God's, you move even *further* from his will and his goal. This is scary. You may not even realize you are straying away from God's purposes for you, but "a man who strays from the path of understanding comes to rest in the company of the dead" (Proverbs 21:16).

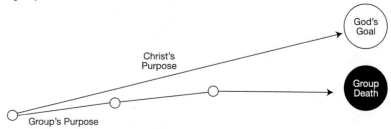

This can be rather demoralizing. How can your group ever get back on track with God's purpose? The answer comes from God's Word: "You can make many plans, but the Lord's purpose will prevail" (Proverbs 19:21, NLT). When you repent and return to him, somehow God's grace and power fill the gap, cover over your multitude of sins and waywardness, and bring you back in line with his purposes.

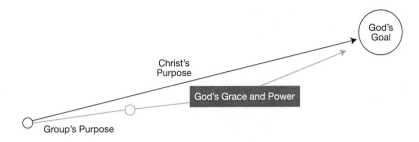

When your hearts are soft, God adjusts you to bring you back into his will. He doesn't adjust himself to *your* will; he adjusts you so you can conform to *his* will. If your group has been going your own way, repent. Ask him to reveal his will for your group: his values, mission, goals, and plans for you. Obey him. "Then you will understand what is right and just and fair—every good path" (Proverbs 2:10).

MAKE GOD-SIZED GOALS AND PLANS!

Healthy small groups make missional, God-sized goals and plans. God is a missional God and we as his followers are called to be a missional people. Living out his mission takes intentionality and effort, however.

Think about these statements:

> **A God-sized goal is something so big that if God isn't in it, it's destined to fail.**

- If your goals are what you can accomplish on your own as a group, they are not God-sized.
- God-sized goals and plans should make your group say, "there's no way we can do that!"
- God-sized goals and plans should drive you to your knees.

God makes an incredible promise to your small group. In fact, it's more of a dare: "God can do anything, you know—far more than you could ever imagine or guess or request in your wildest dreams!" (Ephesians 3:20, *The Message*). So why not make some God-sized goals and plans as a group? What do you have to lose?

HOW TO DISCOVER AND COMMIT
TO GOD'S GOALS AND PLANS FOR YOUR GROUP

Use the following steps to discover and then commit to God's goals and plans for your group. Use the "Small Group Goal-Setting User's Guide" in Appendix D with your group to go through this process together.

[Important note: Unfortunately, many groups skip the first seven steps and start with tactics. They are "Indiana Jones" groups, just making it up as they go. They are reactive rather than proactive, which is foolish and unproductive. Follow the steps in order and you will move forward in health!]

Before You Begin:
Start with yourself and your core team.

You should move through the process outlined below as a core team first before you discuss it with the whole group. Read Jesus' prayer for his followers in John 17:6-19, and use it as a model to pray for those in your group.

Step 1: Pray together.

Set aside a time devoted to group prayer. Be creative, using scriptural prayers and psalms to surrender your planning to God. Consider Psalms 20; 33; or 40. Or rewrite the believers' prayer in Acts 4:24-30 in your own words for your group. You could study the Israelites' prayer in Nehemiah 9, and then pray together with this as a model. For a prayer that focuses on your mission as a group, look together at Paul's request for prayer in Colossians 4:3-6. Use it as a guide for praying together for what God has called you to do as a group.

You will, of course, pray throughout this whole process, asking God for his wisdom as you set goals and make plans, but it is important to set aside a time up front to consecrate all this to him.

Step 2: Analyze where your group is now.

Before you can plan for the future, you need to have a clear understanding of where you are right now. Jim Collins refers to this as "confronting the brutal facts."[3] Ask the group, "What are the brutal facts of our current reality?" Collins says, "When you start with an honest and diligent effort to determine the truth of your situation, the right decisions often become self-evident."[4] Combining this analysis with prayer (#1) will clarify your goals and plans and make this process easy.

A valuable tool used in many businesses is a S.W.O.T. analysis. Take time to brainstorm the group's Strengths, Weaknesses, Opportunities, and Threats.[5] If you use this tool, be careful to not get bogged down in the details. Keep this simple in order to determine the brutal facts of the group right now.

Step 3: Recognize your group's values.

What does the group value? This is the starting point because what you value determines everything else. Kingdom values include things like relating to unchurched people, discipleship, serving others, and leader development.

Your group's values may come from your church or your small group ministry. Ask a church pastor or the groups point person for these values. Examples of small group values may include relationships, authenticity, confidentiality, respect, availability, worship, serving others, sharing our faith, and multiplication.

Step 4: Discover your group's vision.

A vision is a big-picture view of what your group exists for. It's a picture of a preferred future and the destination. Whereas your mission (#5) is a verb, your vision is a noun. Jesus gave the early church their specific vision: They would be his witnesses in Jerusalem, Judea, Samaria, and eventually the whole world. That was their picture of his preferred future.

Your group's vision should be a reflection of your church's vision statement. (It may be exactly the same.) You should not need to spend a lot of time here. [Warning: if your group's vision is radically different from your church's vision, you need to pray more and determine that it's indeed from God.]

Step 5: Determine your group's mission.

A mission is the business with which a group is charged. It is your marching orders—what you are sent to do. Notice the verbs, the calls to action, in the commission Jesus gave us: "Go and make disciples of all nations, baptizing them in the name of the Father and of the Son and of the Holy Spirit, and teaching them to obey everything I have commanded you" (Matthew 28:19, 20).

Your group's mission should be tied to your church's mission statement, but it will probably not be exactly the same. Your group has a *specific* calling from God to accomplish his vision and purposes. What has he called your group to achieve within your church's bigger mission? Keep your mission statement (as well as your vision statement) short and memorable.

Step 6: Clarify your group's goals.

Think in terms of what a "win" for your group might look like. Your win simply clarifies your mission. North Point Community Church uses three questions to help them (and their groups) clarify their win:

- *What do we want people to become?* This question points at the *result* of your efforts as a group. North Point decided they wanted their people to "be growing in their relationship with Jesus Christ."[6]
- *What do we want people to do?* In other words, how will people become what we want them to become? The answer to that question for North Point was to pursue three vital relationships: to grow in their intimacy with God, to grow in community with "insiders" (their neighbors inside the faith), and to grow in influence with "outsiders" (neighbors outside the faith).[7]
- *Where do we want people to go?* North Point uses a simple example of

Little League batters, many of whom have not yet figured out that their goal is to get runners to cross home plate. So, what does "home plate" look like for your group members?

These clarifying questions will help you write a clear goal for your group, but of course they do not replace listening to God and discovering his goals for the group. Make your goals SMART[8]:

Specific
Measurable
Attainable
Realistic
Timely

Step 7: Develop your strategy.

Now it's time to make plans based on your values, vision, mission, and goals. This step answers the "how" question. How will we carry out our goals and get to our win? What's our strategic plan? Sample questions include:

- When and where will we meet? How will we reach out to and relate to non-Christians in our spheres of influence?
- Who, where, when, and how will we serve others together?
- How will we involve the children?
- How will we care for and minister to one another?
- What is our strategy for discipleship?
- What else will be involved in growing spiritually together? Accountability? Subgrouping? Ministering together in pairs?

These questions are much easier to answer, of course, when you have already done steps 1-6. Most importantly, remember that "you can make many plans, but the Lord's purpose will prevail" (Proverbs 19:21, NLT).

Step 8: Employ your tactics.

Tactics are the lowest level of planning. They are the very specific procedures or expedients you use to carry out your plans and to reach your goals. Tactics are dynamic and short-term. They tell you how you will accomplish your plans. Your tactics may include:

- Hosting schedule
- What time you will meet
- How specifically you will encourage one another in your daily relationships with God
- Who will make phone calls
- Who will bring food
- Who will lead the children
- Where you will serve this month

Tactics are where the rubber meets the road, so it's time to go with the plans you've made . . . with one additional vital step.

Step 9: Put it all in writing.

Be sure to make all of the above part of your written agreement or covenant (a copy of a Small Group Covenant is in Appendix C). Keep it handy to discuss regularly. (We ask our groups to bring it out to discuss, reevaluate, and amend three times a year). You can also find lots of other small group agreements and covenants with a simple and careful web search.

Some argue that a signed covenant is too formal and could inadvertently shut down a group, but I've never seen that happen.[9] Just be careful not to overly formalize the process or use of the covenant. It is not a legal document each member must sign in their own blood. It is not to be used to bludgeon people who do not comply. Be careful with those in your group who tend toward the legalistic side of things (you know who they are, unless it's you, and then everyone *else* knows who it is!).

Rick Howerton suggests five benefits of utilizing a group covenant:

- It will give the group an agreed upon purpose and vision
- It is a road map to arrive at a desired destination
- It is a framework for managing potential conflict
- It creates healthy boundaries to function in
- It eliminates unspoken expectations

HOW TO USE GOALS AND PLANS TO KEEP YOUR GROUP HEALTHY

Once you have your goals and plans in place, it's time to utilize them effectively. I know of groups who went through this process and came up with great plans, and then never looked at or talked about them again. The problem is that without clear objectives, you will aim at *something,* and that something may not be too good.

One day on a group mountain bike ride, I was flying through a fast downhill section when I spotted a large tree just off the trail ahead of me. I thought to myself, "That's a big tree. You don't want to hit that tree. Better stay to the right of that tree . . . tree . . . tree . . ." *Wham!* I hit the tree. Fortunately the only thing damaged was my ego. As I dusted myself off and checked out my bike, I noticed plenty of room to the right of the tree. But that tree was like a magnet. I couldn't steer away from it. Why? It goes back to an old adage: "What you look at is where you'll go."

Remember my previous mountain biking example? You must keep your eyes on the path ahead of you and not become distracted with things that are not on the trail ahead. It's easy to do what I did on my bike and get fixated on a feature off the path and end up hitting it. Instead, "let your eyes look straight ahead, fix your gaze directly before you" (Proverbs 4:25). "Look neither right nor left; leave evil in the dust" (v. 27, *The Message*).

There are lots of distractions that will take your eyes and mind off the path and away from the goals you've set as a group. As a leader, you need to differentiate what is on the trail and what's not. As a Christ-centered group, "keep your eyes on Jesus, who both began and finished this race we're in. Study how he did it. Because he never lost sight of where he was headed" (Hebrews 12:2, *The Message)*. God's goals and plans are a way for you as a group to fix your eyes on Jesus.

Your group covenant defines your trail

When new people join your group, talk to them individually and informally after the meeting, letting them know you have a simple covenant as a group to keep you focused on your group's goals. Let them know they will have input on any changes you need to make the next time you discuss it as a group.

If a group member asks, "Why don't we do this or that?" (translation: "Why can't we do it *my* way?") you can point to the group's covenant and respond, "This is who we are. We all agreed on this together." The needs of the whole group and its God-given values and mission are bigger than any one person. A person who thinks the group revolves around him or her can bring down the whole group.

One of the women's groups at our church was really struggling when we first conducted our healthy small group evaluation. In fact, though Gail is a good leader with an incredible heart for God, her group scored the lowest of all our groups on the evaluation. The good news is that Gail wanted to learn how she could improve the health of the group. I met with her and coached her in some specific areas and she attended a workshop on developing goals and plans.

The first thing Gail did was to meet with her group and start the planning process. She used a guide I wrote called *Launch into Community Life* to help her group walk through the planning process together. Several months later, she wrote me the following e-mail:

> Over the last couple months, we've *doubled* our group with the addition of four new members! We started with the *Launch* materials today and this is great stuff! Clearly, you were "led by the Spirit" when you put it together!

You know, for several months I've been clinging to Isaiah 40:31: "But those who wait on the Lord will find new strength. They will fly high on wings like eagles. They will run and not grow weary. They will walk and not faint." Now this group is flying! The progression illustrated in the verse, from flying to running to walking, is obviously slowing down, but the message to me was: Regardless of how swiftly or how slowly things are going, if I remember to "wait on the Lord" he will allow me to *keep on going*. And once again, he has proven himself faithful to his word!

Thanks for all your encouragement and leadership training, direction, and guidance . . . not to mention your prayers! I'm excited to find out where the Lord is going to lead this group of women!

That was more than a year ago. Today, one of the new members Gail mentioned in her letter is stepping out to launch her own new group. She has benefitted from the authentic community of a healthy small group where she has grown as a Christ follower and developed as a new leader. And I believe that was God's plan and goal for the group all along.

Goals and plans are not the panacea for every small group malady, but I have found a huge correlation between groups that set and maintain goals and plans and overall group health (see Appendix B for the findings from our evaluation). As I've worked with unhealthy groups, I've found that the process of developing goals and plans as I've outlined in this chapter has helped those groups get healthy in all the other areas. Wisely using a group covenant will get your group back on the path of Christ's purposes for your group and will help keep you on the right path that will lead you to accomplish the goals God has for you.

THE PROACTIVE GROUP'S
CHECK-UP

1. What does your score on this vital sign tell you about your group?

2. Look at the questions for which you scored a 4 or 5. How specifically have your goals and plans helped your group to be healthy?

3. Now look at the questions for which you scored a 1 or 2. Why did you score low for this attribute? What obstacles are in the way to your group being healthy for that attribute?

4. Look back over the chapter and find principles that address your weakest areas in being proactive with goals and plans. List some ways you can employ these principles:

5. Finish this statement: To become healthier as a group by developing written goals and plans, the first thing I or our group needs to do is . . .

Pray about what you've written here with your pastor or coach.
He or she is eager to support you and help you and your group become or remain healthy.

VITAL SIGN #5
A Healthy Group Lives in Authentic Community

When I first started attending church services, I was alone and a brand-new Christ follower. I lived by myself and had no family in the area. My only acquaintances were people I worked with, most of whom were not Christians. I read through the gospels and the Book of Acts, but had no idea how to incorporate my new beliefs into my everyday life. God had filled the void in my heart, but I sensed something else was missing. When I walked through the door of that church's building that first Sunday, my hope was that I would make friends with Christians, grow in my new faith, and find direction for my life.

As I walked through the front door, an older couple named Harvey

> **God uses Christ-centered community to change lives.**

and Shirley greeted me warmly and asked me about myself. Then they invited me to their house for iced tea on their back porch. And before the service concluded, they introduced me to some people my age, who in turn invited me to their small group. I don't think I've ever felt so accepted.

When I got to the house for that first small group meeting, I drove around the block three times before finally parking my car and summoning the boldness to walk into that stranger's home. I don't remember what kind of snack was served, what we studied, or the prayer requests shared that night. But I do remember feeling very, *very* good about this group of people, and I wanted them in my life.

Over the next couple of months, I enjoyed doing everyday things with these people. These weren't just once-a-week-at-the-meeting acquaintances, but *real* friends who invited me into their lives. This is exactly what I was hoping to find as a new Christian. I didn't know what to call it back then, but I was searching for biblical community.

A week later, two guys from the group, Paul and Eric, met with me to talk about where I was in my new faith. They asked more questions than they provided answers, but they took me to God's Word as we talked about how I could grow in my faith.

At one group meeting after I met with Paul and Eric, I shared that I was confused about God's will for my new life. Now that I was "a new creature in Christ," what was I supposed to do? I wondered out loud if I was in the right career. The group encouraged me and prayed with me to know God's will.

Within a month of joining that small group, the company I worked for went through a takeover and my whole department was eliminated. I went to the group that night and told them what had happened. "What do I do now?" I asked. Again, they supported me and challenged me to seek God's direction. I sensed that God wanted me to use my passion for writing, and they urged me to pursue it. When I was offered a seemingly great leadership position in a Chicago firm, they continued to help me seek God's will. When I turned down the offer, they were there with me, supporting me through a tough decision. Then when I started packing up my apartment to move to Cincinnati to attend seminary, they came and helped me load the truck.

It was hard saying goodbye to these friends God had brought into my life, but I knew he put them there for a *season* and for a *reason*. I ventured out of my comfort zone with a new relationship with God and a community of friends I knew would continue praying for me.

WHAT IS HEALTHY COMMUNITY?

Community is not an organization; community is a way of living: you gather around you people with whom you want to proclaim the truth that we are the beloved sons and daughters of God.[1]
- *Henri Nouwen*

Nouwen provided what I believe is an extraordinary definition of healthy Christian community, one I will work from throughout this chapter. Let's break down his definition.

Healthy Community Is Not an Organization

Community is part of God's nature. Gilbert Bilezikian teaches this eloquently in his book *Community 101*. The Trinity, he says, is the original community of oneness.[2] It is the very essence of who God is and who we are through his creation. Some of Jesus' last words were a prayer about his deep desire for his followers to be one, just as he and the Father are one (John 17:20-26). Jesus experienced perfect community—divine oneness—which he passionately desired for his followers.

As we read through the Book of Acts, it's evident that Jesus' prayer was answered: "All the believers were one in heart and mind" (4:32). Unfortunately, Bilezikian points out, the effect eventually wore off, so the growing church needed to be constantly reminded of its true nature as Christ-centered communities.[3] So do we! Oneness is vital to carrying our Christ's mission.

Your job as a leader is not to *create* community; it already exists in God and how he created you. Your job as a leader is to help your group *enter into his community*. Throughout this chapter, I will share some ways you can enter into an authentic community of oneness.

Healthy Community Is a Way of Living

Community is not so much a purpose as it is the *environment* where Christ's purposes are carried out. Back in high school biology we learned to use a petri dish to grow all kinds of bacteria and mold. But nothing much grows in an empty dish. When you add the culture (agar), however, bacteria grow like wild! Or think about a tree. Without an environment— fertile soil, air, sunlight—it cannot grow. But in a healthy environment, a tree will grow strong and tall and reproduce itself many times. Every-thing needs an environment in which to grow, including Christians. Our environment is Christian community.

For the early church, community was a way of life. One passage every preacher uses when teaching on community is Acts 2:42-47, which illustrates beautifully how these early believers lived life together in Christ-centered community. I'm struck by how devoted these believers were to one another on a daily basis. They met and worshiped together *daily* (Acts 2:46). They served one another *daily* (Acts 6:1). They studied the Scriptures *daily* (Acts 17:11). They encouraged one another *daily* (Hebrews 3:13). And the Lord added to their number *daily* those being saved (Acts 2:47).

Small groups nudge us a little closer in the right direction toward being a day-to-day kingdom community, but if we're not careful it can just move us from the routine of a once-a-week meeting to the routine of a twice-a-week meeting. That's still a far cry from the kind of daily Christ-centered community experienced in the New Testament church. For your group to experience true community as a way of living, some paradigm changes may need to take place, which I'll address in the next few pages.

Healthy Community Has a Kingdom Purpose

Christ-centered community provides just the right environment —indeed the *only* environment—in which Christ's mission of reconciliation is effectively carried out. Again, Acts 2:42-47 provides the perfect illustration. Verses 42-46 describe a vibrant, healthy, Christ-centered community life in the early church. Verse 47 then shows the result. Their community life had the effect of "enjoying the favor of all the people," and because of this, "the Lord added to their number daily those who were being saved."

A woman named Debra responded to one of my blog posts about living in community:

Small groups often divide the church into cliques. The group forms, bonds, and new people stand a chance of joining them. The more groups there are, the more segregated the church. New people see this right away, feel like an outsider, and don't go back.

I feel sad for Debra and anyone who has experienced closed, cliquish, inward-focused groups. A healthy community is never a closed clique. It is open, inviting, welcoming, and missional.

In his classic book, *Small Group Evangelism,* Richard Peace wrote:

In a successful [healthy] small group, love, acceptance and fellow-ship flow in unusual measure. This is the ideal situation in which to hear about the kingdom of God. In this context the "facts of the gospel" come through not as cold propositions but as living truths visible in the lives of others. In such an atmosphere a person is irresistibly drawn to Christ by his gracious presence.[4]

"Holy huddles" is the term some have given the unhealthy small groups Debra described. However, the problem is not in the huddle itself. Every successful team needs a safe place to put our arms around one another, take a short breather, and encourage one another before running the next play to accomplish the team's mission. But that's just it; the group exists not just to huddle but to be the hands and feet of Jesus in our world. (I'll address this more in the next chapter.)

A good small group leader finds a balance between huddling up *and* doing mission. It's not an "either-or" proposition. Learn to live in the genius of the "and." Our mission flows out of our love for one another. When Jesus prayed that his followers would be "one" with one another, he was describing real community (John 17:20). Why? "To let the world know you have sent me" (v. 23).

HEALTHY COMMUNITY TAKES G.U.T.S.!

Community is often described as something safe and comfortable, a place "where everyone knows your name and they're always glad you came." While that's true, healthy community isn't always nice and clean. In fact, it can be downright messy! It takes G.U.T.S. to live in real, Christ-centered community. I'll use that acronym to describe specifically what I think healthy community in your small group should look like.

Healthy Community Is ... Genuine

When I was about ten years old, I made friends with two brothers in my neighborhood, Tim and Jeff Ward. Perhaps because I did not have a brother living at home, or just for fun, I told them I had a twin brother named Mark. We would be playing Wiffle ball, and I'd go home, change clothes, and come back as Mark. To help the ruse, I batted right handed as Mike and left handed as Mark. At first Mike was a better batter, but Mark steadily improved (which is how I became a decent switch-hitter). After a week or so, they grew suspicious, asking me questions like why we rode the exact same bike (our parents were too poor to afford two bikes) or why they never saw us together (because we only had the one bike!). When they came to our house, only one of us was ever around; the other had a game, choir rehearsal, or was at another friend's house. Then one day, Jeff asked my mom where Mark was. "Who's Mark?" my mom asked. The gig was up.

Why do so many of us pretend to be something we're not? I think it's because we're afraid people won't accept us for who we really are. So we put on a mask that hides the real us. We wear these masks at church, too—the one place we should be accepted for who we are. Someone once said "There's more lying on Sunday morning than any other day of the week." That could go for Thursday night at small group as well.

Real discipleship can only happen in an environment of authenticity. If we cannot be real and admit our faults and frailties to one another, we cannot grow beyond where we are. But when we build an environment where we can be real with one another, sin loses its death grip on us. Because people love us "anyway" we have the encouragement we need to battle against Satan's attacks. The accountability of our friends helps us live the life we want to live but can't live by ourselves.

How do you make your group more genuine? Over the years I've discovered the following principles:

1. *It Starts with the Leader.* Group leaders set the tone for appropriate transparency. This starts with your relationship with God. When you have an intimate relationship with God and are sharing honestly and openly with him, you are more able to open your life to others.

2. *Develop Bonds of Trust.* Note that I used the words "appropriate transparency" above. You do not want to share your deepest, darkest sin the first time you meet together. That would erode trust. As you work on your covenant (see Chapter 4), discuss the vitality of confidentiality. Group members must be able to trust others in the group for authenticity to take hold.

3. *Teach a New Way of Living.* Recognize that this may be a new way of life for many people, even long-time churched folks. Help them relearn how to do this, be patient with them, love them anyway when they don't get it quite "right," and dialogue about what authentic community looks like and how it is God's design for your group.

4. *Share Your Stories.* Especially in newer groups, I always ask everyone to draw and then share a time line of their life, zeroing in on the highs and lows and most significant events. Explore ways for people to talk about their histories and what made them who they are today. Self-disclosure is not just a one-time event, however. Use ice-breaker questions to help participants tell their stories.

5. *Don't Force It!* Don't push anyone who is not yet ready to share. Just build the trusting environment in which they can share and give them the time they need to jump in. If you push too hard, you may tear down trust. Some people require an extended amount of time to establish trust, which isn't a bad thing. Continue to affirm and love them, asking God to give them the ability to be more open.

6. *Receive and Affirm.* When people open up and share genuinely about themselves, be sure to let them know they've been heard. Affirm and encourage them for their boldness and vulnerability. This will go a long way in not only making that person feel valued and loved by the group, but will pave the way for others to muster up the boldness to share.

7. *Confess Your Sins to One Another.* Note that this is purposely and strategically placed in the number seven spot for developing genuine authenticity. Once you have built an environment of trust and affirmation, people will more naturally take off their masks and confess their sins to one another.[5] In a couple's group, try sub grouping by gender to build even more opportunity for confession and accountability.

8. *Pray for One Another.* James linked confession with praying for one another (James 5:16). Praying with and for one another brings us into fellowship and welcomes Christ's presence and power into our community. As your group learns a new way of living that involves trust, self-disclosure, affirmation, and confession, prayer becomes richer and more powerful. Perhaps that's one reason that when people in the early church worshiped and prayed together, things started shaking!

9. *Speak the Truth in Love.* The apostle Paul included "speaking the truth in love" as a vital part of building up the body of Christ and growing to become more like Christ (Ephesians 4:11-16). Note again that the order of these principles is essential. We win the right to speak the truth in love by building an environment of trust, self-disclosure, affirmation, confession, and prayer. Speaking the truth in love does not come naturally and is not "politically correct." But if you want to grow in your relationships with Christ and one another, you can't look the other way when a brother or sister is making lousy choices. Learn how to care enough to confront sinful behavior in an environment of unconditional love and with God's grace. As you begin love-based truth-telling in your group, you may want to first talk with your coach or a pastor from your church. Most

---

Practical ideas to make your group meetings more genuine

- Don't plan to start on time. If you open your meetings with Bible study questions, you're prioritizing the curriculum over the individuals. Plan on a casual start to your group by asking people about their day or week.
- Include food! Food seems to break down walls of resistance. Eating with your group around a table helps to build a tight-knit community.
- End on time, but don't end on time. When you finish the "official meeting time," make sure to be done in time for group members to hang around and enjoy each other's company.
- Plan for fun. Set aside the agenda one night and enjoy a pot luck, grilling burgers in the back yard, or a game night. Or go bowling. Or hang out at the park. Hold a chili cook-off. Just be sure to plan it during the time you normally gather since group members have prioritized that time each week.
- Plan extra-group activities. Go on a camping trip or to the lake. Go out to eat on Sunday after church. Pick a random Friday night and have a girls' night out. If you have children, ask the dads to take care of the kids that night. Then switch for the next week and ask the moms to watch the kids for a dad's night out. Several times, the dads in our group watched all our kids together at the church's gym, and I think we had more fun than our wives! (But don't tell them.)

---

importantly, bathe the situation with much prayer, and possibly fasting. And remember, if you can't speak the truth in love (and with the person's best interest at heart) then you're not ready to speak. Keep praying!

10. *Have Fun Together!* Healthy, genuine community should be exciting and fun! Laughing together builds friendships and can even build trust and set the stage for deeper discussions. [Use some of the ideas found above to build fun into your group meetings.]

Our groups at Northeast know how to have fun. Many vacation together regularly, enjoy neighborhood barbecues together, and go to sporting events together. One men's group took a retreat weekend away and attended a college football game. While tailgating, they found out some other tailgaters were celebrating a birthday, so they spontaneously sang. Later they played football against some younger tailgaters and, they were proud to report, "we kicked their butts."

"Love each other with genuine affection" (Romans 12:10). How genuine is the community in your group?

Healthy Community Is … Unconditional

Here's our clear command for living in community: "Accept one another, then, just as Christ accepted you, in order to bring praise to God" (Romans 15:7). How has Christ accepted us? "God demonstrates his own love for us in this: While we were still sinners, Christ died for us" (Romans 5:8). If we accept one another in our small groups the way Christ has accepted us, we will accept them despite their sins, flawed personalities, annoying behaviors, and questionable hygiene!

Small groups are "grace places." We accept people where they are right now. But we hope and pray and encourage and love and study and admonish so that they will grow beyond where they are. Remember, small groups do not make disciples. Disciples make disciples. And small groups do not hurt people. Hurting people hurt people.

I can almost hear people yelling as they read this, *But you don't know So-and-so in my group!* This is important: Just because you accept one another in a small group does not mean you have to accept people's bad behavior or poor choices, and you should never let people take advantage of you or the group. Wise leaders develop boundaries for behaviors, but they handle people with grace. (By the way, much has been written about how to handle members' bad behaviors and difficult personalities in small groups. I've listed some excellent resources at the end of this book.)[6]

The bottom line is that accepting and loving one another unconditionally is a vital part of living in healthy community. How is your group doing at being unconditional?

Healthy Community Is … Tangible

In authentic community we care for one another in *deeds*, not just words. Four men illustrated tangible community when they carried their paralyzed friend to Jesus in the second chapter of Mark. They broke down all the barriers, including some guy's roof, to get their friend the help he needed. Normal people don't do that. It's not rational. But as Heather Zempel points out, "people who understand the community of God are not rational. They embrace the crazy idea that when two or more are gathered, God is truly there and the supernatural can happen."[7]

Real, tangible caring for others is transformational. Zempel goes on to say, "This guy walked away with new faith and new legs because of the commitment of four friends. Their extreme commitment to bringing their friend into an environment to meet Jesus resulted in extreme healing."[8]

Years ago I was in a small group in which a young woman was separated from her husband. The group rallied around, and when she needed a vehicle, Heidi and I decided to let her use our second car, since Heidi did not work at the time. A few weeks later, our situation changed and Heidi needed transportation, so another couple in our group lent us one of their cars, deciding they could walk if necessary. My neighbor stopped me one day and asked about the shuffling around of cars in our driveway. When I explained, he was blown away by how we took care of one another.

Many small groups operate only in the realm of the mind, which is evident in what they are sometimes called: "small group Bible studies." When study is all they do, these groups overlook clear statements in the Scriptures they are studying, such as "Knowledge puffs up, but love [active love] builds up" (1 Corinthians 8:1) and "Do not merely listen to the word, and so deceive yourselves. Do what it says" (James 1:22).

In Romans 12 the apostle Paul provides very practical instructions for healthy, tangible community life. Study it as a group sometime and apply the instructions to how you live together in community. "Don't just pretend that you love others. Really love them" (Romans 12:9). How well is your group doing at loving one another tangibly?

Healthy Community Is ... Sacrificial

Jesus said, "The greatest love is shown when people lay down their lives for their friends" (John 15:13). Real Christian community is sacrificial!

Consider the following statements about how we should live in community with one another:

- "Be devoted to one another in brotherly love. Honor one another above yourselves" (Romans 12:10).
- "Carry each other's burdens, and in this way you will fulfill the law of Christ" (Galatians 6:2).
- "Submit to one another out of reverence for Christ" (Ephesians 5:21).

I sense a need to call a "time out" and face the brutal facts. Much of today's church and what we call "community life" is far from sacrificial. Lay down our lives for our small group friends? First let's get them to *show up!* Our work, our kids' schedules, even our church activities compete for our attention. Ask most people how they are doing, and you'll get a standard one-word answer: "Busy!"

The normal reaction many small group leaders and members make to this busyness is to *lower* their commitment to their small group. "Let's meet every other week rather than weekly. That way, people will be *more* committed to the group." I have never seen this work. Lowering your commitment level will not make you more committed. We have moved so far away from the authentic, devoted, self-sacrificing community of the early church! Consumerism has replaced commitment. Today, it seems, "Christians want change without challenge, strength without suffering, community without commitment."[9]

Once again, we must relearn how to live in healthy, sacrificial community, as God created us to live. A good start may be to understand one simple biblical truth: "we belong to each other," not to our jobs, possessions, favorite TV shows, social media, kids' activities, or, well, you fill in the blank.

When your small group becomes something to squeeze into a packed, hectic schedule—when you have to "find the time" for the important people in your life—then relationships are not your top priority. Something's out of whack. Perhaps what's urgent has taken the place of what's truly vital in your life.

Jesus commanded his followers to "love each other in the same way that I love you" (John 15:12, NLT). His love was sacrificial. He bled for community. How sacrificial is the community in your small group?

WHY HEALTHY COMMUNITY IS SO VITAL

Remember, a small group does not exist *for* community; it exists *in* community *for* discipleship, ministry, and outreach.

Perhaps my favorite worship services ever happened the weekend of January 2 and 3, 2010. During three services, 112 people responded and came forward to be baptized, most of which were spontaneous decisions. The power of the Holy Spirit was very evident as people lined up.

I was especially overjoyed watching one particular person being dunked. Larry is an ex-cop our church hired for security and to direct traffic on weekends. When he started working for us, Larry would not even come into the building. Larry's a big, rough-talking guy who had no interest in our church or spiritual matters for a long time. We planted and watered seeds and prayed for Larry for years, and it produced fruit.

Out of all the people baptized that weekend, why was I so excited about Larry? One word: *friendship*. "The church" as an organization did not change Larry's life. A program didn't bring him to Jesus. No, God used relational disciples like Tim, Steve, Randy, Pat, Caryn, and many others including myself in natural circumstances and conversations to bring about transformation in Larry's life.

Larry was immersed in water that day because Christ-following friends immersed themselves in Larry's life *first*. If you don't remember anything else from this chapter, remember this:

> **Your ministry and mission
> can never be separated from your relationships.**

The question is, does your group have the G.U.T.S. to enter into this kind of transformational community life? Is your group *genuine* enough to take off the masks and be real with one another? Is your love for one another *unconditional,* accepting one another "as-is"? Is your caring for each other *tangible,* not just with words, but with acts of kindness for one another? And are your friendships *sacrificial,* with a willingness to put others needs above your own?

The small group that took me in as a new Christian had the G.U.T.S. to love me in all these ways, and my life was changed. The same thing happened in Larry's life, as a community of people had the G.U.T.S. to enter into what God was doing in his life. If you want to see lives change, get out of your comfortable, cozy, consumer-driven, closed clique, and have the G.U.T.S. to enter into God's ideal for authentic community life.

THE LIVING IN AUTHENTIC COMMUNITY
CHECK-UP

1. How do you feel about your score on this fifth vital sign? Does it seem to you to be an accurate indication of the community of your group?

2. Look at the questions for which you scored a 4 or 5. What specifically has your group done to be so healthy for each of those attributes?

3. Now look at the questions for which you scored a 1 or 2. Why did you score low for this attribute? What obstacles to authentic community are in the way to your group being healthy for that attribute?

4. Look back over the chapter and find principles that address your weakest areas in authentic community. How can you employ these principles to grow in your relationships?

5. Finish this statement: To develop more authentic community in our group, the most important thing we need to do is . . .

Pray about what you've written here with your pastor or coach.
He or she is eager to support you and help you and your group become or remain healthy.

VITAL SIGN #6
A Healthy Group Ministers to Others

The best college football game ever (in my humble opinion) was the 2007 Fiesta Bowl. It pitted the favored Oklahoma Sooners (the most-winning football program in the nation since World War II) against my favorite team, the Boise State Broncos. It was touted as David versus Goliath. The game was full of spectacular plays, an 18-point comeback by Oklahoma, trick plays, many dramatic, game-on-the-line moments, several unbelievable fourth-down conversions, and a spectacular over-time. Boise State won when the Bronco's Ian Johnson ran in a two-point conversion on a Statue of Liberty play. Then, if that wasn't enough, Johnson proposed marriage to his head-cheerleader girlfriend on national television.

As I watched the end of the game, I wish I could have been in the Boise State huddle as they gathered to call one last-ditch trick play after another. I can imagine the smiles of confidence on the player's faces, the nervous energy, and the "we-can-do-it!" attitude.

> **A healthy group moves outward to make an impact in the world**

What does all this have to do with healthy small groups? Plenty. As I alluded to in the previous chapter, a healthy small group is like a football team that huddles to plan, encourages each other, and rests for a few seconds before running the next play. Huddles have a vital purpose, but nobody has ever won a game in the huddle.

Small groups sometime place too much emphasis on the meeting time, as if it alone defines the group. But it's just the huddle. It is a safe place to encourage one another, build each other up, and minister to one another. It is a time to plan and prepare for the next play. The real action happens when we break the huddle to make an impact.

A HEALTHY SMALL GROUP OVERFLOWS

Did you happen to notice the organization of the previous chapter? It started with my story of how an authentic, Christ-centered community changed my life, and concluded with the story of Larry, whose life was also transformed through community. In the first story I was the recipient of God's grace through a loving community; in the second story, I was part of the transformational community. This is God's strategy for making disciples of all nations; he accomplishes it through disciples in the environment of authentic community.

Blessed to Be a Blessing

We are blessed to be a blessing to others, not to remain in a holy huddle. Abram (Abraham) is a good example:

> The Lord had said to Abram, "Leave your country, your people and your father's household and go to the land I will show you. I will make you into a great nation and I will bless you; I will make your name great, and you will be a blessing. I will bless those who bless you, and whoever curses you I will curse; and all peoples on earth will be blessed through you" (Genesis 12:1-3).

Before Abram could be a blessing, he was told to leave his comfort zone and go to the place that God would show him.

The apostle Peter had to get out of the comfort zone of his boat to walk on water. The apostles left "everything" (their comfort zones) to follow Jesus. Moses, Samuel, David, Matthew, and Paul all became passionately involved in God's kingdom work after they had an encounter with the Living God that forever changed the direction of their lives. Notice that passion is not enough on its own. People in your small group are passionate about many things, but God wants more than our passion. He wants us to be willing to count the cost and actually move out of our comfort zones to live for him. Disciples make disciples. God uses transformed people to transform other people.

Years ago when I worked in downtown Cincinnati, a newspaper called "The Downtowner" interviewed people for a feature they called Miss or Mr. Downtowner. One of the questions for a particular Miss Downtowner was, "What is one thing you'd most like to see?"

"More homeless shelters," responded Miss Downtowner.

Later in the interview she was asked, "What would you do if you won the lottery?"

She said, "I'd buy an island and throw a huge party for all my friends."

Miss Downtowner said she had a passion for the poor, but she wasn't willing to count the cost herself. When provided the opportunity, she would do something for herself and her friends. Miss Downtowner is a sad illustration of many small groups today. Who does your group exist for? This is a decision you must make: to care only for yourselves or trust God and break the holy huddle to engage with Jesus in his mission.

Decision Points

Small groups who settle for safe and comfortable are not healthy and therefore do not grow. (By the way, the same can be said for individuals.) Groups stagnate when they remain in their holy huddles and do not get out on the field to take some holy risks and run some dramatic, game-on-the-line plays. I've discussed the following graph previously:

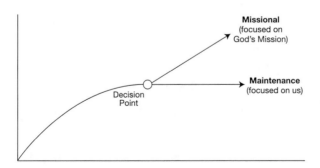

Many groups start in an up-and-to-the-right trajectory. Things seem good. Participants are excited, even if nervously so. New Christians often start their new life in a similar path—getting to know God through his Word, learning what it means to follow Christ, growing fast.

In time, however, that growth slows and plateaus. The newness wears off. Conflicts arise. We settle into routines—often safe and comfortable routines. I've seen this plateaued state have two negative effects on individuals and groups: (1) They stay in this comfort zone for a long time, sometimes for the rest of their lives. They become satisfied with being comfortable. (2) The individual's faith or the group life begins to wane, and the line begins to drop. Often groups at this stage begin to plunge downward—sometimes quickly.

The group comes to a decision point—a time when they must make a vital decision. They can continue to settle for comfort and not grow, or they can decide to do something risky, maybe even dangerous, to get out of their comfort zones. This often means leaving their huddles and going into their communities and the world to make an impact. Individuals and groups come to a number of these decision points during their lifetimes. Each time, they must make a decision to leave their comfort zones to grow.

DEPENDENCE ON GOD

Getting out of your comfort zones to do ministry together places you in a position where you must depend more on God than yourselves. This stimulates growth. It also takes the focus off yourselves and your troubles and turns you instead to think of others first. I shared with my fifteen-year-old daughter recently that when she's in a bad mood that I noticed she is focused on herself and the unfairness of life. The next thing you know, she's exhibiting bad behavior that then gets her into trouble at home, which just compounds her problems. I encouraged her by saying when something external causes her to be upset, do something for someone else: write a letter to encourage a friend or pray for a classmate who does not know Christ, for instance. Why? Because it works!

One of my favorite movies is *Groundhog Day*. Phil, the character played by Bill Murray, keeps reliving Groundhog Day over and over. He wakes up to the same song, goes through the same motions, and meets the same people everyday. That would be quite boring if it weren't for some intriguing character development. Seeing himself turn bitter because of his circumstances, Phil begins using the unique opportunities he has to serve others. His heart begins to change, which finally—without giving away the ending—changes his circumstances. The movie is a good illustration of this basic truth: serving others develops our own characters and changes our hearts.

EMBRACING INTERDEPENDENCE

Besides providing an opportunity for individuals and small groups to get out of their comfort zones and grow spiritually, serving together also causes groups to bond together in stronger relationships. I've grown to know people in my group better and bonded with them more by painting a wall or taking a mission trip together. Something about working on a common task together develops real relationships—and memories. Also, it's just fun to serve together! Squirting one another with hoses as we're (supposed to be) washing cars, laughing with each other as funny things happen as we're serving together, eating together off makeshift tables constructed out of sawhorses and lumber, taking a break on a mission trip in Guatemala to go swimming in a cold lake—these are all fun memories I have of serving with my friends.

Your Covenant (Chapter 4) should include God-sized plans for doing ministry together. It helps you to be intentional and strategic about serving, but remember that it is just a tool, not a contract.

Defining Ministry

Before getting specific about *how* and *where* your group can serve others, I want to quickly define and differentiate some terminology. I did not write one specific chapter on being missional because I consider *missional* to be nearly synonymous with *healthy* when it comes to Christian community. This whole book is about being missional! By *missional* I simply mean that your group carries out Christ's mission together.

Ministry, on the other hand, is the outflow of being missional. *Ministry* usually refers to how you serve and reach people outside your group. (If you've read other TOUCH resources that discuss the four directions of a healthy group, I'm referring to "reaching outward.") *Ministry* has been defined simply as "meeting another's need with the resources God has given you."[1] For Jesus, ministry was completely uncomplicated and natural.

Once as Jesus was en route to a man's house to heal his twelve-year-old daughter, as crowds of people closed in on him, a woman touched the edge of his garment. Dr. Luke tells us that for twelve years this woman had suffered from some sort of bleeding, and no doctors could heal her. As soon as she touched Jesus' cloak, her bleeding stopped and Jesus stopped in his tracks and scanned the crowd.

"Who touched me?"

Peter, who had an explanation for everything, remarked, "Uh, boss, *everybody* is touching you. What are you talking about?"

"No," Jesus said, "Some *one* deliberately touched me. I felt healing power go out from me."

The woman 'fessed up. Luke makes a point of saying the whole crowd heard her explanation and that she had been healed immediately. Now Jesus looked her in the eyes and told her that her faith had healed her.[2]

How did Jesus do ministry? It was all part of the rhythm of his life. The woman was healed because power went out from him. How? Jesus' ministry came out of the overflow of his heart. As I've already pointed out, Jesus spent time alone with his Father, and then in the environment of community, healing power flowed from him. Jesus was perfectly obedient and was always tuned in to his Father.

Another time, Jesus was traveling through all the towns and villages doing ministry as he went, teaching, preaching, and healing. The apostle

Matthew observed that when Jesus saw the crowds, he had compassion on them. *The Message* translation says "as he looked out over the crowds, his heart broke" (Matthew 9:36). Ministry comes out of an attitude of compassion. We serve and share because our hearts break for the people with whom we come into contact. If serving comes from other attitudes such as pride or obligation, ask God to change your own heart first (go back to Chapter 1).

Jeffrey Arnold begins his book, *Small Group Outreach* with these words: "Small groups need to be turned inside-out." Yes they do. As a small group, heed Hebrews 10:24 and "spur one another on toward love and good deeds."

HEALTHY SMALL GROUPS SERVE

After extensive world-wide research of churches, Christian Schwarz reported, "Holistic small groups are the natural place for Christians to learn to serve others—both inside and outside the group—with their spiritual gifts."[3] The one thing I would add to his statement is the word *healthy* before *holistic*. Healthy groups serve out of the overflow of their relationships with God and one another.

We have adopted a culture of serving together in our groups at our church. For many group members it's where they first learn to serve and develop a passion for serving. One of our groups started a ministry that makes and delivers sack lunches downtown on Sundays to serve the homeless. Now, a number of other groups take one week a month serving in this way. Another group started taking roses to widows on Valentine's Day. When this ministry outgrew their group, other groups joined them. Two years ago, one of our couples groups organized a medical clinic that served nearly 400 people and involved a total of 375 volunteers! This group of five young couples with preschool kids is now planning their third clinic for later this year. These are just a few examples of ways our groups serve together. We've found that healthy groups serve, but also serving helps groups become healthier!

Christ came as a servant. As Christ-followers, serving is a reflection of who we are. We do not need any other motive to serve others. Again, it should naturally overflow from our hearts as we live Christ-centered lives in community.

The idea of "servant-evangelism" is popular in many churches. In other words, we serve in our community as a means of witnessing to people. Serving can be a bridge to share the good news, but it is not *why* we serve. One pastor said it this way: "In serving others, salvation is our *ultimate* motive but not our *ulterior* motive."[4] Healthy small groups serve *and* share their faith, not one or the other.

HEALTHY SMALL GROUPS SHARE THEIR FAITH

In the words of small group consultant Alan Danielson, "People are dying and going to Hell and we're worried about who's bringing the enchi-fricken-ladas!" Perhaps you're not comfortable with his word choice, but his point is well taken: "Let us never forget that we will have eternity to eat great food with our fellow Christ-followers. We will have forever to talk about the mysteries of the Bible. We'll have the rest of time to worship God. But we only have now to reach people for Jesus."[5]

Jesus once asked a philosophical question: "Who needs a doctor: the healthy or the sick?" The answer seems obvious, but the implication to your small group is more profound. Jesus then revealed his life mission: "I'm here inviting outsiders, not insiders—an invitation to a changed life, changed inside and out" (Luke 5:31, 32, *The Message*). Matthew's gospel says it a little differently: "I'm here to invite outsiders, not coddle insiders" (Matthew 9:13). Your small group exists for the same purpose: to invite outsiders, not coddle insiders!

> **There will be no one in Heaven who needs to hear the gospel. Evangelism will be obsolete in the afterlife.**

Community-Based Invitations

The apostle John made a riveting connection between community and reaching out to our world: "We proclaim to you what we have seen and heard, so that you also may have fellowship with us. And our fellowship is with the Father and with his Son, Jesus Christ" (1 John 1:3).

For many years, the church has taught an "individualistic invitational style" of evangelism: You, as an individual, go out and share your faith with another individual, and you invite that person to come into a "personal relationship with Jesus" (a phrase that isn't found in the Bible, and is usually interpreted as a *private* decision). The Bible teaches a community-based invitational style. A healthy community of believers ("we") invite people into our fellowship (John's use of "our fellowship" is important; it indicates not just any kind of fellowship, but fellowship that was distinguishably Christian) . . . a Christ-centered fellowship. The implications are:

You, as a Christian, are in Christ-centered community.
↓
You invite others in your spheres of influence into your community.
↓
Because your community recognizes Christ at its center,
when people enter into your community,
they enter also into community with God.
↓
God's Spirit works in the midst of this community
to transform lives and bring people into communion with him.

My friends and I mountain bike a couple times a week because we enjoy the thrill and exercise. But our purpose goes far beyond just having fun on the trails. We pray and look for opportunities to develop relationships with other mountain bikers, often inviting others to join our group as we ride. These rides often turn into longer-term relationships in which we have natural, unforced occasions to move conversations beyond mountain biking. We post our group rides on local mountain biking web sites, and riders often join us.

Through one of those postings, I began an online discussion with Ed, a fellow mountain biker who "just happens" to be my age, lives within a mile of me, and has a son who goes to school with my kids. Ed began riding regularly with our group, and we have become great friends, not only riding together but hanging out between rides. Our cycling group may not look like your small group, but you may have more in common with us than you think. We have formed a community with a cause. We have looked at our interests and skills and where God has placed us, and we have sought God's purpose for us. We are seeing God work in and through our mountain biking community to change lives.

A paradigm change and a new strategy and tactics may be necessary for many existing community or Bible-study groups to break the huddle to go and carry out Christ's mission.

A Community Tactic

Jesus has given us a simple approach for reaching non-Christians in our world. It is repeated often throughout the gospels. It really is, by its nature, an excellent small group tactic, regardless of the type of small group. It's simply:

Come and see . . . Go and tell . . . Come and see . . . Go and tell . . .

The Christian life is not just about coming to Jesus; it's also about going and telling others about him. Your small group is much more than just a "come and see" group; it's also a "go and tell" group. So go and tell what you've seen and heard . . . so that they can come into fellowship with you and see how good God really is! Some groups get stuck in a "come to us" way of thinking. They are somewhat open to people if they make the effort to inquire about their group, but that's all. Our commission, however, is to "go." A healthy group finds a rhythm between "come and see" and "go and tell."

I want to be very careful to not make small group evangelism sound like a step-by-step process or program. It's not! It's a lifestyle. But I have found some helpful principles and strategies that will help you become a "Come and See . . . Go and Tell" kind of group.

It Starts with the Leader's Heart

Leader, you must go first and model this lifestyle for your group members. If they don't see your compassion for lost friends—if you don't even have any lost friends!—it's unlikely they will get excited about going and telling as a group. (I discussed this as an attribute of a healthy leader in Chapter 2. I also wrote about this in much more detail in Chapter 7 of *Leading from the Heart.*) Make going and telling a *lifestyle.* Evangelism is not a program; it's what flows from the heart of a Christian who truly loves God and loves people. As Jim Petersen said, "This kind of evangelism can hardly be called an activity in which one engages on certain occasions. It is *life.* Living itself becomes evangelistic."[6]

Prayer is the Power Cord

Evangelism is a collaborative effort as we partner with God as his representatives. God initiated the reconciliation process between himself and mankind by sending Jesus. But he has now "given us the task of telling everyone what he is doing" (1 Corinthians 5:19, *The Message).* We can't do this without him. God has determined not to do it without us. This human-divine partnership cannot work without the power cord of prayer plugged into the Source.

Paul depended on prayer as he carried out the work God gave him:

Devote yourselves to prayer, being watchful and thankful. And pray for us, too, that God may open a door for our message, so that we may proclaim the mystery of Christ, for which I am in chains. Pray that I may proclaim it clearly, as I should (Colossians 4:2-4).

Here are a few topics you can pray about as you get started:

1. Pray that God will give you his heart for the lost sheep.
2. Ask him for opportunities to go and tell.
3. Ask him to open your eyes to the harvest.
4. Begin praying for people in your circles of influence by name. Make a

list of people you will pray for. (*The Blessing List* from TOUCH is a great resource I often use in groups I lead.) Pray for the needs of people on your list (you may need to ask). Ask God to draw them to himself.

"You're Welcome!"

A healthy small group is open, inviting, and welcoming to new people. Groups must be intentional about not becoming closed cliques. Talk about this often as a group. The "empty chair" is an old standby to help group members remember that the group is open and to invite new people. Leave a chair empty at every meeting and refer to it every once in a while to remind everyone that you still have spaces open to invite others. This is a hard pill to swallow, but I'm speaking the truth in love when I share…

> **If you are not open and willing to reach out to people outside your group, you've missed the point of biblical community.**

Here are the top ten things you *don't* want to hear when you pray for the person who will fill your empty chair":[7]

10. "Lord, please bring someone who doesn't have bratty kids like the ones we can hear right now screaming their heads off in the other room because their parents never discipline them! Amen!"
9. "Lord we need someone who can take over leadership of this small group. Our leader just doesn't have what it takes. Amen."
8. "Our new neighbor has just retired as a professor of theology for secondary education and is putting the final touches on his latest book entitled, *The Right Way to Lead a Small Group*."
7. "Lord, we really haven't had an EGR (extra grace required person) for a long time . . ."
6. "Lord, please fill the chair and make the one Sally is sitting in empty."
5. "God let every one of those 100 people I gave flyers/maps to show up."
4. "Lord, this is the last time we're gonna do this."
3. "Dear Lord, I need another car, so send us a car dealer so I can get a good deal."

2. "Lord, let them have a pool, a recreation room, a home theater, a beach house, jet skis, and the gift of hospitality."

1. "To be honest, Lord, I really like to put my stuff on that empty chair."

Making Your Small Group Less Scary

Some people believe you cannot have authentic community with one another and, at the same time, be welcoming to outsiders. I disagree, but it does take intentionality. How do you not scare off potential new members? How do you integrate them into your groups? Here are a few ideas:

- *Pay attention to natural inviting rhythms.* When is the best time to invite a friend to your group? If your group is in the middle of a six-week study, will it be awkward for a new person to join you? Instead, wait for the beginning of a new study. Is there "stuff" going on in your group that needs to be worked out before inviting a new person? For instance, if you're in the midst of a group conflict, it may not be a good time to ask someone new to join you! Or if you're working through a tender issue, such as a couple's serious marriage problems, deal with that first.

- *Have a plan for when new people show up.* Be prepared to do something fun and non-threatening when a new person shows up. Your group may be at a good-friend or even family level in your relationships, but the new person is an acquaintance at best. So do some things that you would do with acquaintances. Don't expect them to jump right in to the existing group dynamic. Watch out for things like insider jokes. You can share them, but explain the jokes knowing the person probably won't "get it" or see the humor in it.

- *Be authentic.* A tension exists between having a plan for when new people show up and being authentic. Just walk this tightrope the best you can. I've found the best thing to do to break this tension is to talk about it. Say something like, "Ellen, we're really glad you've joined us tonight. This group started two years ago with Bob and Donna and Heidi and me. Jim and Jenny joined us a couple months ago . . ." (This shows Ellen that new people joining the group is normal.). "We've become pretty good friends and well, we have our idiosyncrasies, too. You know, everybody's normal till you get to know them!" (Laughter is a great icebreaker.) Then explain what you've been up to as a group and where you're going. But don't go into a long explanation detailing every aspect of your group. Your guest will figure stuff out as you go. Encourage the members of your group to be themselves. Your guests will find out soon enough who you really are.

- *Be normal.* You're a Christian small group, so it's normal to talk about spiritual things. But it's also normal to talk about sports, work, kids, movies, and so forth. Talk about stuff each of you is passionate about and let guests also see what the group is passionate about. If you have been praying for this person, it's OK to let them know that (without getting overly serious about it).

- *Introduce everyone.* When a group starts, we usually introduce ourselves and tell our stories. When a new person shows up, it's like a new group to them. The rest of the group may have moved past some of the introductory icebreakers that ask you to share parts of your history, but these are very helpful when a guest joins you. "Where did you grow up?" "Who was your best friend growing up?" These and other such questions can help get everyone on the same page faster.

- *Explain (almost) everything.* If you had never been to a small group, what would *you* like to have explained? Of course, don't overdo this, but take a moment to clarify what you do and why. By the way, what seems normal to you may seem odd or confusing to a non-Christian. Be careful not to be condescending!

- *Don't assume* that a guest will or will not read, pray out loud or not, or engage in conversation. Just ask.

- *Have fun!* Almost everyone likes to be part of something fun and as Christians we should be known by having a sense of joy. (See Chapter 5 for some ideas for having fun together.)

Teaming Up

You can become more evangelistic as a group by first supporting one another's efforts. Pray for one another and your non-Christian friends. Leverage other group members' hobbies and interests who may have something in common with your non-Christian friends. Also leverage other group members' spiritual gifts, knowledge, and skills. When my friend Ed started mountain biking with our group, he also met Robby and Dave, among others. Ed has a number of things in common with each of these guys that he doesn't have with me, so they can have an impact in areas that I cannot. Each of them also has spiritual gifts, passions, and skills I don't possess. Ed doesn't realize it, but God has put us together just the way he wants us, so we can show our friend a more complete picture of a Christ-follower.

The good news is you do not have to share the Good News on your own! In fact, you are not meant to do this alone. Evangelism is a community effort. Jesus sent his apostles out in pairs, never alone, to take his message to the cities. They would be there to support and encourage each other and hold one another accountable. Each of us is an important resource for each of the others in our group!

Group Witness

Once you've learned to team up and you're supporting one another's evangelistic efforts, you will naturally develop a group witness. "God never intended evangelism to be an individualistic effort," says Jim Petersen.[8] It's easy to discount or explain away the witness of an individual, but a group witness is nearly irrefutable. As Petersen points out, when someone sees a whole group's witness as the body of Christ, the Holy Spirit stands out as the common denominator. This is true with our mountain bike group. None of us are perfect, but there is a consistency among us and what we value that Ed must notice.

Body Evangelism

In his grand design, God has put your group together in a very unique way and for a very unique purpose in his kingdom. Why is Charlie in your group? Perhaps he has a role in carrying out the mission God has given your group. Each of you has different spiritual gifts, passions, personalities, temperaments, strengths, interests, and circles of influence. God has designed each of those attributes as well. When we combine all our God-given resources, the Holy Spirit can do something totally wild and beyond our imagination—something God-sized.

My wife Heidi makes friends easily and has the spiritual gift of mercy. Evangelism is one of my main gifts. God uses us together to accomplish his purpose. Heidi develops friendships and makes people feel unconditionally loved and cared for. I can explain the good news in understandable ways. Neither of us could share God's story of reconciliation alone. We need one another just as all of us in Christ's body need one another. Jim Petersen illustrates it this way:[9]

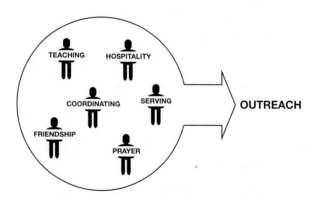

Change the labels to describe the gifts, abilities, passions, and interests of your group members and talk about how you can combine your resources to act as the body of Christ to carry out his mission of reconciliation.

BREAKING THE HUDDLE
WILL MAKE A LASTING IMPACT

One of my favorite scenes is a small group who has helped a friend come to Christ, celebrating together as their friend is baptized. Sometimes it happens in a swimming pool or hot tub of a member's home. Sometimes it happens at the church building with one of the group members baptizing a friend. Either way, it's a fulfillment of 1 John 1:3. The group has proclaimed to this person what they have seen and heard so that their friend could have a relationship with them. Now, this new Christian has a relationship not only with them, but with the Father and his Son, Jesus Christ.

I've seen groups giving high fives and pumping their fists in the air as they celebrate their friend's changed life. You'd think someone had just scored a game-winning touchdown. Of course, none of that would have happened if the group had stayed in the huddle!

THE MINISTRY TO OTHERS
CHECK-UP

1. What does your score on this sixth vital sign tell you about your group?

2. Look at the questions for which you scored a 4 or 5. What specifically has your group done to be so healthy for each of those attributes?

3. Now look at the questions for which you scored a 1 or 2. Why did you score low for this attribute? What obstacles to serving together or sharing your faith are in the way to your group being healthy for that attribute?

4. Look back over the chapter and find principles that address your weakest areas in ministering together. How can you employ these principles to develop as an outward-focused group?

5. Finish this statement: To become a more outward-focused group, the most important thing we need to do is . . .

Pray about what you've written here with your pastor or coach.
He or she is eager to support you and help you and your group become or remain healthy.

VITAL SIGN #7
A Healthy Group is a Discipling Environment

"Thirty years of discipleship programs, and we are not discipled."[1]

Jim Petersen wrote these words in 1993. Now it's been nearly fifty years of discipleship programs, and nothing much has changed. Programs haven't worked, and some would argue that small groups haven't either (more on this later).

Today, many have redefined discipleship into something Jesus would not recognize. Classes, curriculum, models, steps, paths, processes, plans. . . . there's no shortage of creative ideas. Look up "discipleship training" on the web and you'll find plenty of programs

> A healthy group is intentional about discipleship.

and resources you can purchase for your church. Come on! Discipleship isn't that complicated.

All this confusion over discipleship is by design. We have an enemy who wants to steal, kill, and destroy our hearts. He is a master of confusion. Spiritual growth is spiritual battle against all the enemy wants to do to us. The last thing he wants is for us to grow and develop more confidence and power in our faith. So he makes spiritual growth more complicated than it should be.

DISCIPLESHIP HAPPENS

God uses everything in life to transform and grow us: suffering, grief, failures, and many other life circumstances. As I have been writing this book, I've gone through a tremendous amount of emotional pain and spiritual battle. In the midst of it, God called me out for a run one night and spoke to me as clearly as I can remember. He told me this pain is a gift from him. A gift? Really? It doesn't feel like a gift. It feels like a tremendous burden. But I heard him again, *Yes, this is a gift to you. I am using this to develop you into the man I want you to be. I've got this, and I have a purpose for it. Come to me. Trust me.* God is at work in the midst of this painful circumstance. He is present, powerful, and purposeful. What Satan intended to harm me, God is using to grow me.

We often miss what God is doing as we go through the stuff of this life. I've found that I need to train myself to look for the bigger story beyond what I immediately see and feel. God is always at work in the lives of his children, whether we see it or not. He is for me. My job is to trust him.

Discipleship cannot be contained in tidy little boxes. It happens as you and your small group members do life with God and one another. This is God's *Plan A* for the spiritual growth of his people! He pours his life into you and others in your group so that you can overflow into the lives of those who need it. It can be messy, unpredictable, and may seem chaotic, but God is sovereign in all of it.

You've undoubtedly seen the old bumper sticker that says "Stuff Happens," or a slight variation on that. As Christians, we need a sticker that says, "Discipleship Happens." I know that doesn't seem very strategic, but we *can* be strategic about developing the environment and leadership where it will happen. I'll discuss how you can do that later in the chapter.

Discipleship ≠ Small Group Bible Study

Jesus is our perfect model for how to disciple people in a small group. He modeled a relationship with God as he walked with his disciples and as they did life and ministry together. He didn't teach them how to pray in a classroom environment. He went away regularly to pray, and when his disciples asked him about it, he taught them. He did not do evangelism training and then send them out to share their faith. They saw his heart for lost people, he modeled compassion, he sent them out in pairs, and then he taught them when they returned.

Many times in small groups we equate discipleship with what we study. Jesus, however, did not hold a weekly Bible study with his disciples. He lived out God's living and active Word, and then applied the Scriptures with them as teachable moments sprung up. Many years ago, I came across this cartoon:[2]

"I've asked Peter to give each of you a copy of this week's discussion questions."

This cartoon is funny because it is so ludicrous that Jesus would disciple his followers like many small groups do today. Jesus, as well as the early church, lived in deep relationships with one another, providing the perfect environment for discipleship to happen naturally. Small group Bible study does not equal discipleship. I agree with what John Eldredge said: "You can do some study till you're blue in the face, and it won't heal the brokenhearted or set the captives free. We come to learn; we leave. It is not enough."[3]

Welcome to First Pharisaical Church

The Pharisees of Jesus' day would feel at home in many of our churches and groups. They would enjoy the deep theological Bible studies and pious prayers. They'd appreciate the discussions about honoring God, and they'd be happy that few conversations deal with the heart. This was one of Jesus' biggest beefs with the Pharisees. They dealt with a lot of external matters, but they totally missed the heart. A Christ-centered small group is an environment where disciples can connect with God and connect with one another's hearts.

When Satan fights against you and your family, who will stand with you in the battle? Who will encourage you to keep going? Who will love you despite your mess ups and messiness? Who will care enough for you to hold you accountable to the spiritual disciplines you want to pursue? It's unlikely that the person sitting next to you in your small group will do these things unless your group is what Eldredge calls a "fellowship of the heart." He says,

> Going to church with hundreds of other people to sit and hear a sermon doesn't ask much of you. It certainly will never expose you. That's why most folks prefer it. Because community will. It will reveal where you have yet to become holy, right at the very moment you are so keenly aware of how they have yet to become holy. It will bring you close and you will be seen and you will be known, and therein lies the power and therein lies the danger.[4]

Does that describe your small group? Does your group ask much of you? Does it expose you? Does it reveal where you have yet to become holy? Is it an environment where God can fill, fix, and change your heart? Is it real?

Years ago, I was part of a group of men who were each committed to become men after God's own heart. Each of us was dealing with our own issues. Some needed to deal with an addiction or idol in their lives. Some wanted to become better husbands or fathers. Others wanted to become more disciplined in their daily relationship with God. This was much more than just an accountability group. We were men who deeply cared about one another's hearts (although as men we would not have put it that way), enough to speak the truth in love when necessary. We could, and did, call one another and meet even if it was 3 A.M. We each grew in our relationships with God as the Holy Spirit did his work in our community. Today, nearly twenty years later, many of these men are disciple-making leaders whom God is using in his kingdom.

A Disciple's Definition of Discipleship

If you could ask Jesus' original disciples to describe discipleship, they would talk about a rabbi. In their context, a disciple was someone who was totally committed to a particular rabbi. Usually, disciples literally lived with their rabbi and followed him everywhere he went. Communal living was absolutely necessary for living as a true disciple. Teaching happened more by example than by words as you lived with the person each day. The purpose was to become "like the teacher" (Luke 6:40).

Rabbis taught in *yeshivas*, groups of disciples who would have passionate discussions over some aspect of life and what the Hebrew Scriptures said about it. They would wrestle with the texts together in order to understand God's view on how they should conduct their lives. Most Jewish boys had memorized large amounts of Scripture by the time they were thirteen in preparation for their Bar Mitzvahs, so they did not need to study what God's Word said as much as how to apply it to life.

Rabbis used no written curriculum or agenda for their multi-year discipling experience. Their curriculum was life itself. The rabbi observed the daily life of his disciples and then asked probing questions to initiate discussion about observed behaviors. A disciple could also initiate conversations by raising an issue regarding his observation of the rabbi's life or some life issue or question.

Jesus adopted the rabbinic style of discipling his followers, but he altered it quite a bit from how it was normally carried out. John 15:12-17 illustrates seven ways Jesus was counter cultural as a rabbi. As you look through this list, consider how his pattern for discipling applies to your small group.

- Rabbis trained their disciples in the law. Jesus' discipleship was based on grace: "My command is this: Love each other as I have loved you" (v. 12).
- Rabbis required a short-term commitment. Jesus called his disciples to total surrender of their lives: "Greater love has no one than this, that he lay down his life for his friends" (v. 13).

- Rabbis required their disciples to serve them in practical ways (think, "wax on, wax off . . ." from *The Karate Kid*). Jesus treated his disciples as friends: "You are my friends if you do what I command. I no longer call you servants" (vv. 14, 15).
- Rabbis did not call their disciples. A potential disciple would ask a rabbi if he could follow him. It was up to the rabbi to say yes or no. But Jesus called his disciples: "You did not choose me, but I chose you . . ." (v. 16).
- Rabbis focused on head knowledge so that their disciples could eventually train others in the Jewish religion. Jesus called his disciples to actually do something: "I . . . appointed you to go and bear fruit— fruit that will last" (v. 16).
- Rabbis taught their followers to be dependent on them. Jesus taught his disciples to be dependent on God: "Then the Father will give you whatever you ask in my name" (v. 16).
- Rabbis used a top-down approach to discipleship. While his methods were based on his authority, Jesus taught his disciples from a mutual-discipleship model: "This is my command: Love each other" (v. 17).

Jesus' rabbinic style of discipleship is not just attending a weekend church service and meeting in a once-a-week small group; it is 24-7 living. It happens in your quiet time, work time, family time, and play time . . . every day.

21ST CENTURY DISCIPLESHIP

How can we accomplish discipleship like Jesus did it in today's culture? We may not be able to take a time machine back to 30 A.D. or change the culture in which we live, but we can look to Jesus and apply the ways he discipled into our context today.

Here are ten vital factors for developing Jesus' rabbinic model of discipleship in your group:

1. Commitment

A first-century disciple was committed to God, his rabbi, and his yeshiva. More importantly he was committed to being a disciple. Commitment is the starting point, and we cannot have healthy, disciple-growing groups without it. This commitment requires a cost. Jesus required surrender if you were to consider following him. Three times in Luke 14, he told his followers that if they did not count the cost, they could not be his disciples:

- "If anyone comes to me and does not hate his father and mother, his wife and children, his brothers and sisters—yes, even his own life—he cannot be my disciple" (v. 16).
- "And anyone who does not carry his cross and follow me cannot be my disciple" (v. 27).
- "Any of you who does not give up everything he has cannot be my disciple" (v. 33).

What is Jesus saying? Consumers cannot be disciples. It takes a costly commitment to him. In a healthy small group today, members commit to (1) Christ, (2) the group, and (3) mutual discipleship.

Committed to Christ — David Watson says, "A disciple is a follower of Jesus. He has committed himself to Christ, to walking Christ's way, to living Christ's life and to sharing Christ's love and truth with others."[5]

What does it look like to be committed to Christ? It may involve a number of lifestyle choices:

- Involvement in daily study and contemplation of God's Word
- Prayer, including listening to God
- Pursuit of God through other spiritual disciplines such as fasting and solitude
- Living with integrity, that is, living life God's way, not mine
- Using the gifts God has provided to build up his body

You could probably add other items to this list. But be careful to not make this commitment legalistic. This should not become a list of do's and don'ts that group members must follow. You are simply defining what this group is all about—discipleship—and you are clarifying the commitment involved.

I recently had a conversation with Bob, a small group leader at our church. Bob has a very intimate relationship with Christ that exudes from him. He told me about his frustrations with some of his group members who are not very committed in their relationships with Christ. As Bob shared this with me, tears welled up in his eyes. Bob wants so much more for them, and his heart aches that they don't seem to be growing—or even want to.

I shared with Bob that as leaders we often need to move from expectations to expectancy. Often we expect group members to live up to certain standards, like reading their Bibles every day or fasting once a month or coming prepared to group meetings. Those expectations can lead us to judgment. Instead, we need to move to expectancy, which means we accept people as they are, but we have a hope that they will grow closer to God. Expectations are about me. I expect them to live up to my standards. Expectancy is based on trusting God to do what only God can do in a person's life. It means I will be praying for that person constantly. I will invest into his life. I will encourage. I will offer to disciple him. I will ask if he'd like accountability for what he commits to.

Jesus does not force his way into our lives to make us grow. He stands at the door and knocks.[6] And then he waits for us to respond to his voice and to open the door for him to come in. There is no legalism or judgment here. There is simply an invitation and an expectancy that we will respond to him. Now, imagine you are in the room with a group member who seems uncommitted to Christ and to growing in him. Your job is not to answer the knock on the door for him. Neither is it to push him to the door. It's to lovingly encourage the person to respond and to show him the way by the way you respond to Jesus.

Committed to the group — When you start a new group, or when a new person joins your small group, make the commitment to discipleship as clear as possible. This is where your goals and plans come in (Chapter 4).[7]

Of course, setting the bar high like this has a trade off. Some people will not join a group that requires high commitment. But for those who accept the challenge, you will make disciples. I imagine it was tough for Jesus to watch the rich young man walk away, but Jesus was committed to making disciples, not attracting crowds of consumers.

Committed to mutual discipleship — Mutual discipleship means we are committed to helping one another grow in our faith. This is what Paul meant when he said that Christ's body should grow and build itself up in love as each part does its work" (Ephesians 4:16). In the healthiest groups, members are not only committed to their own spiritual growth (a more acceptable form of consumerism), but to helping others grow. The rest of these factors describe what's needed for mutual discipleship to happen in a group.

2. Observability

One of the values that made rabbinic discipleship work is that disciples lived an observable life with one another. Because they literally did life together, there was no hiding. As a disciple, you could expect the rabbi to ask you at any time, "Why did you do that?" These interactive "behavior formation" questions provided much more than just imparting how-to formulas. Rather, they helped disciples develop wisdom and discernment.

Many of us avoid being exposed, but a healthy small group is a place where we can be fully seen, fully known, and fully accepted anyway! Healthy community should reveal where each of us has yet to become holy.

Obviously, this is not so easy to achieve in our individual, unshared-life society, but today's technology can actually help, if we learn to use it wisely. Texts, tweets, Facebook, and other social media can help make our lives a little more observable to others. It's not exactly communal living, but it's a step in the right direction.

How can you make your lives more observable to one another? As I discussed in Chapter 5, it includes sharing your stories and your lives regularly, doing life together between meetings as much as possible, and building accountability into same-gender relationships within the group. It takes building trust with one another and a desire to know each other and be known.

Let me pause here for a moment, because I mentioned, almost in passing, same-gender relationships, but I don't want to speed past this. I believe that real, observable discipleship happens best when men meet with men and women with women. Accountability, confession, and admonishment happen more naturally when I'm with the guys without the women around, and vice versa. Does that rule out couples or other mixed-gender groups? No. But if you want to see authenticity and discipleship explode, subgroup by gender for prayer, sharing, and application. In couples groups I've led, I've regularly gathered the guys together for breakfast or lunch to hang out and develop more accountability. For example, tonight the guys in my group are meeting to watch the number-one and number-two-ranked college football teams play. My guess is that this fun time with the guys tonight will help them be more observable to one another . . . and this will help some eventually reveal where they have yet to become holy.

3. Personal Responsibility

Discipleship happens when individuals are spending time with God each day. They're reading, studying, and meditating on God's Word in their own personal quiet times. If the only time people open their Bibles is during the small group meeting, that's not enough! That's not healthy. That's not real discipleship.

People must be responsible for their own spiritual growth, with the support, encouragement, and accountability of others in the body of Christ. So often, I hear long-time church-goers say, "I just need to be fed." It's natural for baby Christians to say this (see 1 Corinthians 3:1, 2; 1 Peter 2:2; Hebrews 5:13), but as we grow, we begin to learn how to feed ourselves. In fact, when we are mature, we ought to be feeding others

(Hebrews 5:12, 14; 6:1). We grow not by being fed, but by feeding ourselves on the meat of God's Word and then by becoming spiritual parents who feed others.

My four kids are all teenagers now. When we sit down for dinner tonight, not one of them will ask me to cut up their meat or feed them. In fact, each of them knows how to prepare a meal for the rest of us. When our neighbor's babies are around, they can feed them their mashed peas. This is no big deal, of course. It's just a natural part of growing up. If my kids told me, "I just need to be fed," I'd be worried!

What is your small group teaching people to do: depend on others to feed them or feed themselves and then others? Develop an environment where you are encouraging people to feed themselves as they commune with God each day.

When group members show up at a meeting after communing with God through the week, the Holy Spirit is not a stranger when he shows up! Group members come prepared to share with one another what God is doing in their lives. All week, God has been pouring into them. Now, when they meet together, he overflows from one life into another—mutual discipleship. A whole group that is spending daily time with God naturally overflows into the lives of others outside the group as well. It's in these overflowing groups that God adds to the number daily those being saved!

4. Wrestling Together

Disciples who are spending time in God's Word throughout the week come together when the group convenes to wrestle with the Scriptures together . . . to determine together how to live out God's Word in their lives. A healthy small group does not just study the truth of Scripture (for more head knowledge) and it does not just "do life together" in a nice little social club. In a healthy small group, the truth of God's Word and real life come together and members grapple with that. They take a passage of Scripture, perhaps one they read during the previous week, and talk about how to actually make that happen in real life situations.

What's this look like? Let's say Philippians 4:6 really spoke to someone in their time with God during the past week. A group member reads that verse (and often other verses around it): "Do not be anxious about anything, but in everything, by prayer and petition, with thanksgiving, present your requests to God. And the peace of God, which transcends all understanding, will guard your hearts and your minds in Christ Jesus." The leader may ask, "So, when do you tend to get anxious about things?" Several people say they get anxious at work, especially with recent layoffs. A Core Team Member asks, "So how could you go to work tomorrow and live this verse out? How can you keep from being anxious about the situation?" Everyone enters into this dialogue, perhaps sharing ways they have depended on Christ's power rather than becoming anxious. Others share what a struggle that is in real life. The group wrestles with this and then someone suggests they pray together for members who are struggling with anxiety at work. Because this is a group of friends, several enter into the struggle by sending notes of encouragement throughout the week.

This is not a typical Bible study using printed curriculum. But I am also not trying to create a whole new method for small group discipleship. Wrestling together with the Scriptures can happen in a variety of ways:

- *Use a Reading Plan* — A wide variety of daily Bible-reading plans are available in churches and on web sites. Have your group choose a plan and agree to all use it. That way, everyone is on the same page, so discussion can be more dynamic.
- *Focus* — Some groups focus on less Scripture, say a chapter a day, and read through books of the Bible. I like this method for groups who want to commit together to reading through certain Bible books and getting more in-depth than the previous option.
- *Intently Focus* — An even more focused way of getting into God's Word is to read just one chapter throughout the week, but to read it each day from different versions; use commentaries, study notes, and other tools; journal; and use other methods to contemplate and pray through God's Word. Usually more mature Christians enjoy this

method, but if you use it, also have some "lighter" questions ready to go when visitors come.

- *Get topical* — Use a topical Bible, concordance, or chain reference to study a topic of interest thoroughly. During the week, group members study the topic on their own and come to the meeting prepared to share. What topic? The shepherd-leader should try to discern this with lots of input and ownership from the group. Again, a dependence on the Holy Spirit to guide the group's direction and discussions is vital.

- *Be Devotional* — One of the best experiences I had in a group was using a simple devotional, like *Our Daily Bread* or *My Utmost for His Highest.* Members read the Bible passages as well as the devotional thoughts each day, and come to the meeting prepared to share.

- *Read What You Want, but Just Read!* — I've found that in many groups individuals find their own methods of Bible reading that fit their time schedules, personalities, and level of spiritual maturity. The important thing is that everyone keeps their commitments to getting into the Word each day, and the group encourages one another and keeps each other accountable to that. Each group member comes prepared to share one thing that jumped out at them or where they heard God speaking to them. The group leader and other members ask questions and enter into the dialogue, sharing how God has used that verse to transform their lives, for instance. This option may be called "cha-ordic": living as a group on the edge of chaos with enough order to give you a pattern for discipleship.

Remember the purpose of getting into the Word together? It's discipleship, not just more head knowledge. In other words, you're setting out to be transformed, not just informed. The group should wrestle to apply the Scriptures together, bringing the truth of God's Word into real life.

Do small groups who wrestle together over the Scriptures ever do a typical Bible study using a printed curriculum? Sure. For instance, a group for parents of teens at our church has used good video-based studies on the topic. But—and don't miss this!—the material is not why they meet. Growing in their relationships with Christ is about more than just being good parents of teens. So they emphasize everyday discipleship. They take time to talk about what they are hearing from God on a regular basis. The men and women meet separately for some iron-sharpening-iron conversations. And then they also wrestle with what they are learning about being godly parents of teenagers. This is not just a nuance. It can be a big paradigm change for many groups who see themselves as "study groups."

5. Wrestling with Christ

As you wrestle as a group with God's Word, you wrestle with Christ. He is present with you, remember? He is the Word made flesh. He is the Truth. His Spirit will help you understand everything in the Scriptures. When you come across difficult passages to understand or put into practice, ask him to step in and help. When people in your group are broken or hurting, walk with them to Jesus. He is the only true source of healing power. When people are struggling or going through crises, let them know that God is at work in the midst of this. The role of the group leader is not to fix people's problems or answer all their questions. It is to guide them to our Healer, Counselor, and Comforter.

Don't forget that Christ is the real leader. You are not a rabbi who has your own yeshiva. Your role is to make disciples of Jesus. Lead like Paul, who said, "Follow my example as I follow the example of Christ" (1 Corinthians 11:1). I discussed how to do this in Chapter 1.

6. Leading and Being Led

While Christ is our real leader and Good Shepherd, believers need a human shepherd, too—someone who invests into their lives, cares about their souls, listens to their hearts, and guides the way. One of the commitments group members must make is to be led. A problem in many small groups is a lack of understanding of the biblical principle of authority. Christ is the Head, and all authority belongs to him. He gives a measure of his authority to leaders, and we are called to submit to those godly authorities. Many groups decide on everything by voting. I've seen other unhealthy groups in which individuals would not set aside their own expectations and priorities for the good of the group. Discipleship cannot happen in that kind of environment. A healthy group needs a healthy leader who is not passive or afraid to lead. Review Chapter 2 for much more on healthy leadership.

7. Teaming Up

Using a true definition of discipleship, a leader can effectively disciple no more than two or three others. Others can watch and listen and grow, but if you are to invest into people's lives, you must limit your span of influence. As I showed in Chapter 3, that's what Jesus did. Break out of the mindset that you can disciple ten or twelve or more. Share leadership with a core team and develop an environment for mutual discipleship to happen (core team members discipling members and members discipling people who come to Christ as a result of the group's outreach efforts).

8. Planning

Get strategic and build an environment (authentic community) where discipleship can happen. Discipling may be messy and somewhat chaotic, and it may be more up to the Holy Spirit than what you can possibly do as a human leader, but you can and should develop plans. God is not a God of disorder, but of peace (1 Corinthians 14:33). Review Chapter 4 for more on making plans, and be sure to harness your church's discipleship pathway if your pastoral leadership has established something for members to move through.

9. Mutuality

One-on-one discipleship happens best in the environment of authentic community. Several years ago I was in a group with five other guys who met together weekly to discuss the Bible passages we read through the week and how they applied to our lives. I met separately with one younger guy in the group who I discipled in more specific ways. As he dealt with several tough circumstances, I walked by his side and cared for him.

Since much of our spiritual growth occurs through hardships and trials, we need others to walk with us through our valleys. Their encouragement and love help us see what God is up to. They care for us and help us carry our burdens. They pray for us and with us and pick us up when we fall. As I've walked through a recent valley in my life, I've learned so much through my godly friends who have given me wise counsel. They've stretched me, challenged my thinking and actions, and emboldened me to make hard but wise choices. I'm a better man today not just because of the valley, but because of my friends who walked with me during difficult stretches along the way. Review Chapter 5 for more ideas about how discipleship happens in the environment of authentic community. Just remember, we don't study discipleship, we experience it in community!

10. Ministering Together

Ministry is the great discipleship activator. People grow best when they get out of their comfort zones to serve alongside their friends or to share their faith with their group's prayers and support. Do we grow spiritually in order to minister to others or do we minister to others as a way to grow in our faith? Yes! Ministry and discipleship have a mutually beneficial relationship (explored in Chapter 6).

DISCIPLESHIP IS A LIFETIME PROCESS

The ten discipleship factors are all parts of this lifetime process. Which of these are you doing well? Which do you need to improve as a group? Perhaps your group is already an environment where mutual, over-flowing discipleship happens. If it is, way to go! If you need to make some adjustments or even a paradigm change, it's best not to force or impose these changes upon the group. Get their ownership. "A Guide to Move Your Group toward Yeshiva Discipleship" is included in Appendix G to help your group decide together how you will implement a healthy process for discipleship.

"Go and make disciples …" That's the mission for your small group. And it will happen when your group is healthy: Christ-centered, with a healthy leader and core team, who have goals and plans, live in authentic community, and do ministry together.

THE DISCIPLING ENVIRONMENT
CHECK-UP

1. What does your score on this last vital sign tell you about your group when it comes to discipleship?

2. Look at the questions for which you scored a 4 or 5. What specifically has your group done to be so healthy for each of those attributes?

3. Now look at the questions for which you scored a 1 or 2. Why did you score low for this attribute? What obstacles to discipleship are in your way for that attribute?

4. Look back over the chapter and find principles that address your weakest areas in discipleship. How can you employ these principles to develop as an disciple-making group?

5. Finish this statement: To become a group where people are naturally growing in their faith, the most strategic thing we need to do is . . .

Pray about what you've written here with your pastor or coach.
He or she is eager to support you and help you and your group become or remain healthy.

CONCLUSION
The Fruit of Healthy Small Groups

A healthy apple sapling grows, becomes a strong tree, and produces fruit. Some of that fruit falls to the ground where its seeds can embed themselves to produce new apple seedlings. The same holds true for people: A healthy child grows, matures to

> **Healthy groups produce fruit and increase in number.**

adulthood, and starts his or her own family. It's not difficult to see that healthy things grow and reproduce themselves. It's the natural order of the way God created his world to operate: Be fruitful and increase in number . . . multiply.[1]

Small groups that are healthy in each of the chapters discussed in this book will, under most conditions, grow and multiply. It just comes naturally. This happens in different ways:

- A core team member feels a tug from God to start a new group
- A group grows too big
- The meeting time becomes inconvenient for one or more members
- Group members don't agree with the direction of the current group
- Group members move into a new life stage (for example, a couple in a newly married couple's group has a child)
- Group members have specific needs not being met in the present group (for example a couple in a group begins raising grandchildren and starts a "grandfamilies" group)
- Group members move to a new neighborhood (or even a new area of the country)

- Group members meet new friends with whom they have something in common and start a new group around that commonality
- Group members make new friends with people who need Jesus in their lives

All of these examples have occurred at our church. Sometimes the group does not view it as a *birth* or *multiplication,* but God uses all kinds of life circumstances (or new opportunities) to expose his kingdom to those who have not yet seen it. Celebrate what God is doing regardless of how it happens!

One of the most "reproductive" leaders at our church is Laura. Her group has birthed many times, so I asked her to lead a training session on how to multiply a group. She admitted to me she had no idea what to teach others. "It just keeps happening!" she exclaimed. Laura's group was healthy in all seven vital signs, so growth and multiplication happened naturally.

One power source and two accelerators!

As I've already suggested, these vital signs describe a process for becoming a healthy group—a transformative process that begins with Christ at the center. All the other vital signs depend totally on this one. Apart from Christ at the center, a group cannot be healthy or produce any fruit!

HEALTH REQUIRES VITAL SIGN INTEGRATION

Don't think of these vital signs as a cafeteria plan where you pick three or four out of the seven and voila, you're healthy. No, it's how you integrate all of them into your group that determines your health. It's much the same as the health of the human body. If your blood pressure and pulse rate and cholesterol are all good, but your blood sugar is too high, you're not healthy. Something's wrong and requires attention.

However, we have noted two accelerators for group health: maintaining written goals and plans and sharing leadership (with a core team).

At Northeast, we found a direct correlation between these two vital signs and all the others. We also found that when groups became healthier in these two vital signs, that it helped them become healthier in the others as well. So be sure to incorporate the other healthy vital signs into your goals and plans, and share leadership in developing and implementing them.

One of the best ways for you to utilize this book and improve the health of your group is to do what the groups at our church did. I encourage you to assess your group using the Healthy Small Group Evaluation in Appendix E or online at this web address:

http://www.touchusa.org/free-small-group-health-assessment

I also highly suggest taking the assessment again in about six months to reassess the health of your group. Use this to diagnose how well you've progressed and where you can still improve. As you continue growing as a group, use the "Checkup Sheets" at the end of each chapter to discuss how your group is doing.

One last thing. There is one more vital sign of a healthy small group: *perseverance*. Anything that is great, whether a healthy family, business, church, or anything else, owes its success to persevering through tough times. Even the healthiest of groups go through tests and trials. Remember that God works for the good of those who love him and are called according to his purpose . . . and that applies to your small group as well as to you as an individual. Keep going. Don't give up. Don't short-circuit what God is doing in and through your group. Because "perseverance must finish its work so that you may be mature and complete, not lacking anything" (James 1:4).

**Healthy small groups
—groups that stay connected to Christ—
produce much fruit. And this is to the Father's glory.**

Healthy Small Group Resources

Vital Sign #1: Christ-Centered

Looking Upward: Helping your group members develop a supernatural relationship with God, by David Finnell (TOUCH, 2005)

Christ's Basic Bodies: Embracing God's presence, power, and purposes in true biblical community, by Ralph W. Neighbour Jr. (TOUCH Publications, 2008).

The Relational Way: From small group structures to holistic life connections, by M. Scott Boren. See especially Chapter 2. (TOUCH Publications, 2007).

Experiencing God: How to Live the Full Adventure of Knowing and Doing God's Will, by Henry T. Blackaby and Claude V. King (Broadman & Holman Publishers, 1994).

A God-Centered Church: Experiencing God Together, by Henry T. and Melvin D. Blackaby ((Broadman & Holman Publishers, 2007).

Vital Sign #2: Healthy Leader

Leading from the Heart: A Group Leader's Guide to a Passionate Ministry, by Michael C. Mack (TOUCH Publications).

I'm a Leader . . . Now What? How to Guide an Effective Small Group, by Michael Mack (Standard Publishing, 2007).

8 Habits of Effective Small Group Leaders: Transforming Your Ministry Outside the Meetings, by Dave Earley (TOUCH Publications, 2001).

Leadership by the Book, by Ken Blanchard, Bill Hybels, and Phil Hodges (William Morrow and Company, 1999).

How to Lead a GREAT Small Group Meeting, by Joel Comiskey (TOUCH Publications, 2010).

52 Secrets of Small Group Leadership, by Dave Earley and Rod Dempsey (TOUCH Publications, 2012).

Spiritual Leadership, by J. Oswald Sanders (Moody Press, 2011).

When Leadership and Discipleship Collide, by Bill Hybels (Zondervan, 2007).

Vital Sign #3: Core Team
The Pocket Guide to Burnout-Free Small Group Leadership: How to Gather a Core Team and Lead from the Second Chair, by Michael C. Mack (TOUCH Publications, 2009).

I recommend using *Moving Forward: Helping Your Group Members Embrace their Leadership Potential* (TOUCH Publications, 2005) as a six-session study with your group. While I wrote this guide before we fully integrated core teams into our small group leadership, it is written with this concept in mind. As the title of the book implies, it will help you move forward as a group, growing in your faith and leadership potential together. The sessions are written to prepare group members to step up and launch new groups as God calls them.

8 Steps to Multiplying Small Group Leaders, by Dave Earley (TOUCH Publications, 2012). While this book focuses on the more traditional apprenticeship/internship model, it provides great instruction for discovering, developing, and deploying new leaders out of your group.

Doing Church as a Team, by Wayne Cordeiro (Regal Books, 2009). While this book is written for church leaders about how to share church leadership, it has many implications for small group leaders as well.

Church Is a Team Sport: A Championship Strategy for Doing Ministry Together, by Jim Putman (Baker Books, 2009). Like the previous book, this is written for church leaders, but it is also written for churches where small groups are vital to how they do ministry.

The Leadership Baton: An Intentional Strategy for Developing Leaders in Your Church, by Rowland Forman, Jeff Jones, and Bruce Miller (Zondervan, 2007).

Vital Sign #4: Proactive
Built to Last, by Jim Collins (Harper Collins, 1994, 1997)

Good to Great, by Jim Collins (Harper Collins, 2001)

S.M.A.R.T. Goal Setting Guide: http://www.goal-setting-guide.com/smart-goal-setting-a-surefire-way-to-achieve-your-goals

PlanoOnline.org: "Conducting a SWOT": http://www.planonline.org/planning/strategic/swot.htm

Vital Sign #5: Healthy Community
Connecting Inward: Helping your group members develop a deep love for one another, by Mark Collins (TOUCH, 2005)

Community Life 101: Getting the Most Out of Your Small Group Experience, by Randall Neighbour (TOUCH, 2005). As part of our community strategy, I buy these by the case and give new group members a copy.

Community 101: Reclaiming the Local Church as Community of Oneness, by Gilbert Bilezikian (Zondervan, 1997). This is heavy on the theology side and light on the practical, so it's not for everyone.

Refrigerator Rights: Our Crucial Need for Close Connection, by Dr. Will Miller and Dr. Glenn Sparks (Willow Creek Resources, 2008).

Building Up One Another: How Every Member of the Church Can Help Strengthen Other Christians, by Gene A. Getz (Victor Books, 1983). This one may be hard to find these days, but it is a classic, in my view. Each of the twelve chapters covers one of the New Testament one-anothers.

Making Room for Life: Trading Chaotic Lifestyles for Connected Relationships, by Randy Frazee Zondervan, 2003).

Connecting: A Radical New Vision, by Larry Crabb (Word Publishing, 1997).

The Safest Place on Earth: Where People Connect and Are Forever Changed, by Larry Crabb (Word Publishing, 1999).

Vital Sign #6: Ministry

Reaching Outward: Helping your group members bring Christ into everyday relationships, by Jim Egli (TOUCH Publications, 2005)

101 Ways to Reach Your Community, by Steve Sjogren (Colorado Springs: NavPress, 2001). This book contains 101 creative ideas for serving and sharing your faith together.

Small Group Outreach: Turning Groups Inside Out, by Jeffrey Arnold (Downers Grove, IL: InterVarsity Press, 1998).

Small Group Evangelism: A Training Program for Reaching Out with the Gospel, by Richard Peace (Downer's Grove, IL: InterVarsity Press, 1985). This book is an old classic, but still contains some of the best practical ideas for reaching out as a small group.

Seeker Small Groups: Engaging Spiritual Seekers in Life-Changing Discussions, by Garry Poole (Grand Rapids, MI: Zondervan, 2003). This book is about how to develop a group specific for spiritual seekers. In my opinion, that's *every* healthy small group!

Living Proof: Sharing the Gospel Naturally, by Jim Petersen (Colorado Springs: NavPress, 1989). The companion video series to this book was, I believe, one of the best ways to teach a small group how to share their faith together. It's hard to find now and dated.

The Externally Focused Church, by Rick Rusaw and Eric Swanson (Loveland, CO: Group, 2004).

The Master Plan of Evangelism, by Robert E. Coleman (Revell, 1963). This book is the classic of all classics when it comes to evangelism and small groups. (Yes, this is Lyman Coleman's brother. The forty-fifth printing of the book in 1987 was dedicated to Lyman and his wife Margaret. If you have never read this book, it's a must-read.)

Vital Sign #7: Discipling Environment
Moving Forward: Helping your group members embrace their leadership potential, by Michael C. Mack (TOUCH Publications, 2005)

All the books in TOUCH Publication's *Spiritual Formation Backpack*:
Welcome To Your Changed Life by Ralph W. Neighbour, Jr.
A Journey Guide for New Believers by Ralph W. Neighbour, Jr.
Beginning the Journey by Ralph W. Neighbour, Jr. and Jim Egli
Encounter God Manual by Jim Egli
The Arrival Kit by Ralph W. Neighbour, Jr.
Mentoring Another Christian by Ralph W. Neighbour, Jr.
Touching Hearts by Ralph W. Neighbour, Jr.

The Relational Disciple: How God Uses Community to Shape Followers of Jesus, by Joel Comiskey (CCS Publishing, 2010)

Organic Disciplemaking: Mentoring Others into Spiritual Maturity and Leadership, by Dennis McCallum and Jessica Lowery (TOUCH Publications, 2006)

How People Grow: What the Bible Reveals about Personal Growth, by Dr. Henry Cloud and Dr. John Townsend (Zondervan, 2001)

Lifestyle Discipleship: The Challenge of Following Jesus in Today's World, by Jim Petersen (NavPress, 1993)

The Disciple-Making Church, by Bill Hull (Fleming H. Revell, 1990). Any book about discipleship by Bill Hull is worth reading. His materials have been very influential on my understanding of the topic.

Renovation of the Heart, by Dallas Willard (NavPress, 2002)

The Spirit of the Disciplines, by Dallas Willard (Harper, 1988)

APPENDIX B
For the Small Groups Point Person:
What Our Small Groups Ministry Learned

"Be sure you know the condition of your flocks,
give careful attention to your herds." — Proverbs 27:23

Several years ago, our senior pastor asked me a simple question: "Are our small groups healthy?" I could tell him all the reasons why I *thought* they were healthy. I could tell a few stories. I could talk about what I had observed. But I could not *prove* our groups were healthy. So we developed a simple diagnostic instrument using an online survey tool and sent it to all our leaders to learn more.

What a paradox! We were attempting to analyze a very relational ministry by extracting cold hard data out of something that's spiritual and communal. Through this experience, we learned a simple questionnaire surrounding small group health is not a perfect science, but the information we gathered was still valuable to help us know the current condition of our flocks and to better diagnose their health.

Brian Jones created a lot of controversy a couple years ago when he wrote that churches should *euthanize* their small groups. Why? Jones reported, "Modern-day small groups are led, for the most part, by people who have attended the church, had a conversion experience, led a reasonably moral life, and can read the study-guide questions, but are not disciples themselves."[1] Many churches have lowered the bar of small group leadership to an absurd level, according to Jones. "If you can read, you can lead." "If you can operate a VCR, you can be a star." The result? Unhealthy, even diseased small groups that Jones says are better off dead.

May I offer a second opinion? Instead of euthanizing their small groups, perhaps church leaders should first do the work of diagnosing the health of their groups. That's what our church has done through the Small Groups Health Assessment found in this book.

We began with *diagnosis* (by sending out the survey), but we didn't stop there. We moved on to *analysis* and *prognosis* and finally to a *treatment plan.* Mark Twain once said, "First get your facts; then you can distort them at your leisure." Be careful not to distort the facts you receive!

Three-Way Analysis

First, we analyzed the findings *as a ministry.* We asked ourselves, "In what areas are we as a ministry strong and where do we need to grow?" We found that two vital signs were particularly vital in the health of all other areas: *Goals and Plans* and *Shared Leadership.* So we focused on these two areas in our workshops, coaching, newsletters, and other ways over the next six months.

Second, we analyzed the findings by *types of groups* (affinities). For instance, we found that our women's groups did not do well with *shared leadership* and our men's groups scored low in *goals and plans.* So our affinity leaders and coaches worked within their groups to strengthen these weak areas.

Finally, we analyzed the findings by *individual groups.* Our coaches and I met one-on-one with leaders to discuss specific actions they could take to become healthier. We visited groups and discussed overall survey findings and information specific to their groups as well, which kept the leaders from feeling overly burdened, knowing everyone in the group was working on healthy changes.

> *You can assess the groups under your care using the online survey on the TOUCH website at http://www.touchusa.org/free-small-group-health-assessment. (A printed version of the survey is found in Appendix E.) We revised our survey quite a bit from the first one we used several years ago. We learned quite a bit not only about our groups, but also about developing surveys. The survey on the TOUCH website is the newest version of our original survey.*

By the way, these "Seven Vital Signs of a Healthy Small Group" are what we came up with at Northeast Christian because they work in our particular culture and circumstances. Yours may be different. You may come up with totally different vital signs or just use your own terminology. For instance, you may notice that I don't have a vital sign specifically for *prayer*. We made prayer an integral part of what it means to be a Christ-centered group. It is also incorporated into the survey questions for several other vitals signs. We also don't have a vital sign for growing numerically or re-producing. I believe those are the natural fruit or result of a healthy group.

Below are some things about each vital sign we learned from our survey and some thoughts for you as the small groups point person. When we first conducted our survey in 2009, we asked respondents to rank, using a 1-5 scale[2], the health of their groups using a series of statements.

Vital Sign #1: Christ-Centered

For the Christ-centered vital sign, we asked leaders to rank their groups on these two statements: "The small group leader and members recognize that God is the real leader of the group (the leaders are stewards of the group)" and "Group meetings are focused on the presence, power, and purposes of Christ in their midst (Matt. 18:20) rather than on curriculum, group issues, individual's needs and desires, etc."

The results showed that we were doing very well in this vital sign. 99 percent of our leaders either agreed or strongly agreed with the first statement. 85 percent either agreed or strongly agreed with the second. While this sounds great, my visits to some of these groups and my conver-sations with group leaders and members often told a different story.

I see two reasons for this difference: (1) Christian leaders often pro-vide the response they think they are *supposed* to give rather than what they actually and honestly perceive. Who wants to say their group is not Christ-centered? (2) Some leaders have a low understanding of what it means for God to be the real leader and for the group to focus on Christ's presence, power, and purpose. For example, a leader might think, *Let's see . . . we pray every time we meet, so we're good on this one.*

Our survey was beneficial on this one, but we learned more about this vital sign by visiting groups and talking to people one-on-one. Our coaching follow-up was also critical to how we interpreted results and helped groups grow in specific areas. That's another great lesson for those of us who oversee small groups in the church.

Vital Sign #2: Healthy Leader

We used four statements to assess the health of the leaders:

1. The small group leaders are growing in their faith by being involved in daily disciplines such as Bible study and prayer.
2. Small group leaders are personally discipling/mentoring or have discipled at least one person over the past three years.
3. Each small group leader has at least one close friend who is not yet a Christ follower, prays regularly for them, and is investing in a relationship with them.
4. The leaders have attended at least one small group leader training event over the past year.

Responses to these questions were not surprising. 85 percent either agreed or strongly agreed with the first question. I made it a priority to pray for, encourage, and disciple the other 15 percent, especially the 3 percent who responded that they disagreed with this statement. (12 percent had "no opinion" or were "neutral" on this one, which makes no common sense to me, but I thought I'd mention it because your results may be similar.)

For the second question, 67 percent either agreed or strongly agreed. 25 percent were neutral. 7 percent either disagreed or strongly disagreed. This one concerned me. Some of our leaders did not see themselves as disciple-makers. They viewed themselves as *meeting facilitators*. We moved forward on this one by redefining the role of leaders for these folks.

For question number three, only 59 percent agreed or strongly agreed with the statement. 30 percent marked "no opinion/neutral." Perhaps they had acquaintances but not "close friends" who were non-Christians. This question showed us that many of our leaders probably see their groups as holding ponds or discipleship centers for Christians, but not as kingdom outposts for missional living.

Most of our leaders (86 percent) attended at least one of our training events during the year. This information, along with my personal relationship with a number of our leaders, told us that our leaders are continuing learners and desire to grow in their competence and skills. (If you don't know your leaders well, do not assume that because they show up to leadership meetings and score high on this question that they are hungry to learn more and grow. Visit with them one-on-one or you may make a false assumption that will not help you in the long run.)

I'm happy with the results of the survey and my personal interaction in regard to the health of our leaders. We still have a lot of room for growth, however. For each of the questions, the largest percentage of leaders responded with a 4 on a scale of 5. My hope and prayer is that many of our leaders will move to a 5 next time.

If your leaders score low on these questions, stop and consider first what *you* can change about your leadership style, not what the small group leaders should change. Do you talk about your times with God and your personal interaction with unchurched friends when you're with group leaders? Do you pray with them about these things when you meet individually and when you train them? Much of the health of your groups begins with your example.

Vital Sign #3: Core Team

Our survey showed a direct correlation between groups who shared leadership as a core team and all the other areas of group health. Unfortunately, a high percentage of our groups did not have core team leadership at the time. The survey question was: "The group is led by a core team of 2-4 members who share leadership. No one is leading alone. "

22 percent strongly agreed; 40 percent agreed; and 38 percent were

neutral, disagreed, or strongly disagreed. From my conversations with leaders, I believe the differentiation between strongly agreed and agreed came down to several factors:

a) The leader had several group members who shared leadership to some degree, but the leaders were still leading alone most of the time.

b) The leader had formed a core team, but was still leading alone—the core team was just a formality.

c) The leader naturally shared leadership with several people from the group, but they had never formally formed a core team.

Because having a core team had such a direct effect on other areas, we spent a lot of time and effort working with groups to make sure they had strong, healthy core teams that were sharing leadership . . . and it worked!

Here are a few of the changes we've made to encourage core teams to share group leadership:

- On our roster forms we now provide a separate section for core team members and another for the rest of the group members. This change illustrates the importance of the core team.

- We include all core team members in leader correspondence, including our regular e-mail to leaders. We treat all core team members as leaders.

- We invite all core team members to our huddles, training, and other leader events.

- We discuss how to work together as a core team with leaders at leadership training events.

- Coaches have been trained to ask leaders about their core teams and coach them in how to effectively work together with them and share leadership.

- I regularly talk with core team members to ask them about their groups, pray for them, and encourage them. I don't push them to multiply. I just treat them as leaders and wait and watch for how God calls them to leadership.

Vital Sign #4: Proactive Leadership

The lowest scores on our healthy small group survey were in the area of *goals and plans*. Only 44 percent of our groups said they had goals, knew their win, and had specific strategies to accomplish them. Even fewer, 37 percent, said they had a written covenant or action plan. This was no big surprise. What was a surprise was how big an effect this had on the group's overall health.

When we filtered out all the groups that do not have goals and plans, comparing the statistics to the original findings in this category, we found that the groups who have goals and plans are healthier in all other areas. The groups who had goals and plans were more Christ-centered, mission-minded, disciple-making, community-building, and reproducing. Because our findings were so clear on the vitality of groups having goals and plans, we spent two main breakout session teaching leaders how to go through the process outlined in Chapter 4.

Percentage by which groups who have goals and plans are more . . .				
Christ-centered	Mission-minded	Disciple-making	Community-building	Reproducing
5%	8%	15%	7%	7%

If your groups score low in *goals and plans,* work overtime to help them see the need for goal setting and long-range plans and watch what happens. You'll be pleased.

Vital Sign #5: Healthy Community

When we conducted our survey, we discovered that two other vital signs had a direct correlation to the level of community. It had nothing to do with how long the group has existed, how small or big the groups were, how young or old the leaders were, or other factors. What made a difference was whether the group members shared ownership and leadership in the group and if the group had written goals and plans. The groups that scored higher in these two vital signs also were relatively healthier in other facets of community life.

Vital Sign #6: Ministry

Groups at Northeast are relatively outward-focused. Serving is a high value in our groups, although evangelism is somewhat lower. Below you'll see how people responded to the four statements under "outward-focused."

	Strongly Agree	Agree	No Opinion /Neutral	Disagree	Strongly Disagree
Christ's mission is the group's mission	28%	49%	18%	4%	1%
The group regularly prays for their lost friends and is sharing their faith with others	24%	49%	18%	9%	0%
The group is intentionally open to new people	37%	36%	21%	6%	0%
The group serves others together	31%	54%	13%	1%	1%

We also found that small groups who maintained written goals and plans had 8 percent higher scores in this area over groups without written goals. This makes sense. Groups without plans or goals never get around to serving others, sharing their faith, or even inviting new people in. These unhealthy groups eventually collapse because they're only focused on themselves.

At Northeast we launch many new small groups with a plan of action for their future using a study I created called *Launch Into Community Life* (TOUCH Publications). This four-week study helps a new group become a healthy, holistic group using studies from Acts 1-6. As the new group discusses how the early church launched into ministry, they develop their own action plan for their future together. We've found that for groups who begin with this material, being outward-focused is much more natural and easy. By launching a group with a core team that focuses on goal setting and outward-living, it becomes part of their DNA.

Vital Sign #7: Discipling Environment

The one thing we learned from our survey about discipleship in our small groups is that we were not asking the right questions at that time. In fact, we discovered that we were not teaching our group leaders and members to disciple one another. Many of our group leaders assumed that if they were conducing a weekly Bible study, it was "discipleship." So, we tweaked the assessment and asked leaders to rank their groups on two very different statements: "Group members are intentionally being discipled" and "The group engages regularly in Bible study and application."

Only 9 percent strongly agreed with the first statement, while 46 percent strongly agreed with the second. I thought it was interesting that 24 percent had no opinion or were "neutral" on the first statement. That told me that many of our leaders did not genuinely understand what it meant to "intentionally disciple group members."

We have made and continue to make big changes in this area. We've moved from an emphasis on study to an emphasis on discipleship, as explained in Chapter 7. We rewrote our new leader training in order to better equip leaders on how to disciple members, not just lead studies. We revised our Small Group Covenant (Appendix C) to include more emphasis on commitments.

Discipleship is the final of the seven vital signs because all the others have such a huge impact on it. In other words, when groups are healthy in the other vital signs, discipleship occurs much more naturally. However—and I believe this is vital for church leadership to remember—a discipleship strategy for groups must also be intentional. This probably includes a simple pathway to spiritual maturity. If your church does not have an easy-to-use pathway, review the discipleship resources TOUCH offers in their Spiritual Formation Backpack and implement something for every member of your groups to move through. By doing this, you'll be equipping and releasing people for ministry just the way Christ commanded (Matthew 28:16-20) *and* your small group ministry will always have enough discipled, Christ-centered leaders for new groups.

OUR SMALL GROUP COVENANT

Our VALUES
The four directional values help us determine what we do as a group.

UPWARD: We agree to be devoted to and developing a supernatural relationship with God by …

INWARD: We agree to be devoted to and developing a deep love for one another by …

OUTWARD: We agree to be devoted to bringing Christ into everyday relationships by …

FORWARD: We agree to be devoted to embracing our leadership potential by …

Our VISION:

God's greatest desire for our group is to become ...

Our MISSION:

Our group exists to ...

Our GOALS:

(Be specific, and us a separate sheet of paper if needed!)

Our COMMITMENTS:

❑ I commit to growing in my relationship with Christ, including my commitment to a regular quiet time that includes Bible reading, prayer, and other disciplines

❑ I commit to the group, including being in attendance whenever the group meets (unless I am out of town or sick – no lame excuses!) and to being an active participant in the group

❑ I commit to mutual discipleship, meaning that we will each help one another grow in our faith together (see Eph. 4:16).

Our VALUES:

I agree to the group values of ...

- *Priority:* I will make attending this group a priority in my life. While I am in the group, I will give the group meeting priority, and if I am running late, I will call ahead.

- *Participation:* Everyone's opinion and questions are respected. (God's Word will be our guide and standard for what is "right" or "wrong," but we will not use Scripture to attack or bully.)

- *Confidentiality:* Anything of a personal nature that is shared in the group stays in the group.
- *Accessibility:* I will make myself accessible to others, especially when there is a need. I give permission to call me at any hour when there is a real and significant need.
- *Accountability:* I will give permission to at least one other person in the group to hold me accountable for the goals I set. (Accountability flows from the person seeking it and will never be forced on a person or used to manipulate.)
- *Boundaries:* I will respect the personal and family boundaries of others.
- *Observability:* I will seek to be open and honest with others. Our small group is a place where we can take off our masks and be truly ourselves, and be accepted for who we are.
- *Ownership:* This is God's group, not mine or the leader's. As parts of the body of Christ, we will all share responsibility for the group's mission, values, and goals.
- *Inclusiveness:* Our group is open to new people. I will pray for and invite people to become part of our community. We will not allow ourselves to become a clique or "holy huddle."
- *Reproduction:* Our group is not only open to new people coming in, it is also open to members being sent out. I will pray for new leaders to emerge and will encourage them to start new small groups.

Our GUIDELINES:

We will meet ❏ weekly, ❏ every other week, ❏ every week per month except the _____ week.

We will meet on _____ (day of the week) from _____ to _____ (time of meeting)

Our meetings will: ❏ be held at _____
(location)
❏ rotate from house to house

Children will:

❏ be part of the group

❏ be involved in some group activities such as the icebreaker, worship, or prayer, but they will be separated for other parts of the meeting

❏ be in their own small group meeting in another room or location (_____ will lead the children's group)

❏ be cared for by a volunteer / paid childcare provider (discuss who this will be, how much they will be paid, and how this will be paid for)

❏ be cared for by a member of the group (one person or rotate?)

Food and refreshments will be provided:

❏ by hosts ❏ on rotating basis ❏ by: _____

I covenant together with the other members of this group to honor this agreement.

_____

Group Member Signature

APPENDIX D

SMALL GROUP GOAL-SETTING USER'S GUIDE

Small Group: _____

Date: _____

Scriptures to consider: Luke 14:25-34; Proverbs 19:21; Proverbs 16:3; Matthew 28:16-20; Ephesians 3:14-21

1. Pray together.

2. Analyze where your group is now (Use a timeline or a "SWOT" Analysis).

"When you start with an honest and diligent effort to determine the truth of your situation, the right decisions often become self-evident."
– Jim Collins

3. Recognize your group's VALUES.
   • Discuss God's values and your church's values.

OUR VALUES:

4. Discover your group's VISION.
   - God's Vision = Reconciliation
   - The vision of our church is (under which we minister):

OUR VISION:

5. Determine your group's MISSION.
   - Christ's Mission: *"Therefore go and make disciples of all nations, baptizing them in the name of the Father and of the Son and of the Holy Spirit, and teaching them to obey everything I have commanded you. And surely I am with you always, to the very end of the age."* —Matt. 28:19, 20
   - The mission of our church is (under which we operate):

OUR MISSION:

6. Clarify your group WIN (Goals).
- What is God calling us to do?
- What do we imagine our group looking like in 1-3 years?
- How can we extend and expand His Kingdom?

OUR WIN:

7. Develop your STRATEGY.
- Short-term goals that help you accomplish your win

OUR STRATEGIES:

8. Employ your TACTICS.
- Specific actions your group will take to carry out your strategy and go for your win.

OUR TACTICS (this is a continuous process):

9. Make your win and strategy part of your COVENANT. Write it below:

OUR COVENANT:

SMALL GROUP HEALTH EVALUATION

For each question below, please circle the number below the response that most closely describes you or your group. Respond to how you would describe your group right now, not what you hope or wish it would or could be. NOTE: You may find that no one response is "perfectly" descriptive. That's OK. Just pick the one that most closely describes your group!

1. When we meet, we recognize that Christ is in our midst.

Not True	Rarely True	True Half the Time	True Most of the Time	True Nearly All the Time
1	2	3	4	5

2. As the group leader or core team member, I am growing in my relationship with God.

Not True	Mostly Untrue	About Half True	Mostly True	True
1	2	3	4	5

3. Leadership is shared in our group. No one person leads alone.

Not True	Rarely True	True Half the Time	True Most of the Time	True Nearly All the Time
1	2	3	4	5

4. Our group has plans for our short-term future (6-12 months).

Not True	Mostly Untrue	About Half True	Mostly True	True
1	2	3	4	5

5. Group members attend our scheduled meetings when they are in town.

Not True	Rarely True	True Half the Time	True Most of the Time	True Nearly All the Time
1	2	3	4	5

6. We are open to new people, invite others to join us, and are welcoming when new people visit.

Not True	Rarely True	True Half the Time	True Most of the Time	True Nearly All the Time
1	2	3	4	5

7. We have an intentional plan for the spiritual growth of group members.

Not True	Mostly Untrue	About Half True	Mostly True	True
1	2	3	4	5

8. Our group's mission aligns with Christ's Great Commission (Matt. 28:18-20).

Not True	Mostly Untrue	About Half True	Mostly True	True
1	2	3	4	5

9. As a leader or core team member, I have a daily quiet time with God, which includes disciplines such as Bible study and prayer.

Not True	Rarely True	True Half the Time	True Most of the Time	True Nearly All the Time
1	2	3	4	5

10. Our group has a "core team" or nucleus of about 2-4 people who share responsibilities in leading the group.

Not True	Mostly Untrue	About Half True	Mostly True	True
1	2	3	4	5

11. Members of our group could tell someone why our group exists.

Not True	Mostly Untrue	About Half True	Mostly True	True
1	2	3	4	5

12. We are a group of real friends.

Not True	Mostly Untrue	About Half True	Mostly True	True
1	2	3	4	5

13. We regularly pray together for lost friends and family members.

Not True	Rarely True	True Half the Time	True Most of the Time	True Nearly All the Time
1	2	3	4	5

14. Individual group members are growing in their faith because of their involvement in this group.

Not True	Mostly Untrue	About Half True	Mostly True	True
1	2	3	4	5

15. We identified the purpose for our group through prayer and/or from God's Word, not from our own opinions or ideas.

Not True	Mostly Untrue	About Half True	Mostly True	True
1	2	3	4	5

16. As a leader or core team member, I regularly find ways to serve group members.

Not True	Rarely True	True Half the Time	True Most of the Time	True Nearly All the Time
1	2	3	4	5

17. Discipling and shepherding group members is shared among two or more people in our group.

Not True	Mostly Untrue	About Half True	Mostly True	True
1	2	3	4	5

18. We have ground rules for how we interact and do life together as a group.

Not True	Mostly Untrue	About Half True	Mostly True	True
1	2	3	4	5

19. Group members regularly share their true selves.

Not True	Mostly Untrue	About Half True	Mostly True	True
1	2	3	4	5

20. We regularly serve people outside our group (quarterly or more often).

Not True	Mostly Untrue	About Half True	Mostly True	True
1	2	3	4	5

21. The lives of people in our group have been or are being transformed.

Not True	Mostly Untrue	About Half True	Mostly True	True
1	2	3	4	5

22. Prayer is a vital part of what we do together as a group.

Not True	Rarely True	True Half the Time	True Most of the Time	True Nearly All the Time
1	2	3	4	5

23. As a leader or core team member, I am a disciple of Jesus Christ (I strive to live as a Christ follower by God's grace).

Not True	Mostly Untrue	About Half True	Mostly True	True
1	2	3	4	5

24. God uses two or more people with different gifts and abilities to team-lead our group.

Not True	Mostly Untrue	About Half True	Mostly True	True
1	2	3	4	5

25. We have a written action plan, agreement, or covenant.

Not True	Mostly Untrue	About Half True	Mostly True	True
1	2	3	4	5

26. Group members are committed to one another.

Not True	Mostly Untrue	About Half True	Mostly True	True
1	2	3	4	5

27. We encourage and support one another in sharing our faith with others.

Not True	Rarely True	True Half the Time	True Most of the Time	True Nearly All the Time
1	2	3	4	5

28. We encourage and support one another to read God's Word individually.

Not True	Mostly Untrue	About Half True	Mostly True	True
1	2	3	4	5

29. We regularly worship God as a group (this may include singing or a variety of other forms for praising and honoring God).

Not True	Rarely True	True Half the Time	True Most of the Time	True Nearly All the Time
1	2	3	4	5

30. As a leader or core team member, I strive to grow in my leadership skills and abilities by reading books, blogs, and/or other resources; getting coaching; and attending training.

Not True	Mostly Untrue	About Half True	Mostly True	True
1	2	3	4	5

31. If an alien showed up at our group meeting and said, "Take me to your human leader," we'd point to two or more different people in the group.

Not True	Mostly Untrue	About Half True	Mostly True	True
1	2	3	4	5

32. Our group's goals and plans are so big that if God is not in them, they are destined to fail.

Not True	Mostly Untrue	About Half True	Mostly True	True
1	2	3	4	5

33. Our group does life together (for example, we get together with others to care for, encourage, pray for, or listen to one another, or just to hang out or play together) outside of meetings.

Not True	Mostly Untrue	About Half True	Mostly True	True
1	2	3	4	5

34. We care for and minister to others outside our group.

Not True	Mostly Untrue	About Half True	Mostly True	True
1	2	3	4	5

35. We have discussed and acted upon a strategy for the spiritual growth of group members.

Not True	Mostly Untrue	About Half True	Mostly True	True
1	2	3	4	5

36. Our group is primarily focused on Christ and his presence, power, and purposes (rather than being focused primarily on content, curriculum, or other things).

Not True	Mostly Untrue	About Half True	Mostly True	True
1	2	3	4	5

37. As a leader or core team member, I am a shepherd (spiritual guide) for the group. People follow my example as I follow the example of Christ.

Not True	Mostly Untrue	About Half True	Mostly True	True
1	2	3	4	5

38. One or more people in our group (besides the leader) could launch and lead a new group.

Not True	Mostly Untrue	About Half True	Mostly True	True
1	2	3	4	5

39. We discuss our goals and plans at least three times a year, making modifications as necessary.

Not True	Rarely True	True Half the Time	True Most of the Time	True Nearly All the Time
1	2	3	4	5

40. Group members love one another sacrificially.

Not True	Mostly Untrue	About Half True	Mostly True	True
1	2	3	4	5

41. God is using our group to reach people who do not yet know Christ or are not yet following him.

Not True	Rarely True	True Half the Time	True Most of the Time	True Nearly All the Time
1	2	3	4	5

42. As a result of group members maturing in their faith, some are becoming or have become leaders in our group or elsewhere in the church.

Not True	Mostly Untrue	About Half True	Mostly True	True
1	2	3	4	5

Now that you've answered all the questions in the assessment, write down the number found just below your answers and record it in the scoring grid on the next page.

1:	2:	3:	4:	5:	6:	7:
8:	9:	10:	11:	12:	13:	14:
15:	16:	17:	18:	19:	20:	21:
22:	23:	24:	25:	26:	27:	28:
29:	30:	31:	32:	33:	34:	35:
36:	37:	38:	39:	40:	41:	42:
Total:	Total:	Total:	Total:	Total:	Total:	Total:
Christ-Centered	Healthy Leader	Shared Leadership	Proactive Leadership	Authentic Community	Ministry	Discipleship

What the totals above reveal about the current health of your group:

Scores of 12 and under for a vital sign indicates an unhealthy situation, which should be addressed immediately using the information from the corresponding chapter in this book.

If your group scored 12 or below for most or all of the vital signs, focus on the first vital sign: becoming Christ-centered. Everything flows out of being focused on Christ's presence, power, and purposes for your lives.

Scores between 13 and 22 for a vital sign indicate your group is doing OK in the area, but there is room for improvement.

If your group scores between 13 and 22 for all the vital signs, your group is not unhealthy, but you could become a lot healthier. Why make the extra effort? Because the next level of group health is where you, your core team members, the other members of your group, and your unchurched friends experience an amazing relationship with God that is transformational and awesome. It's worth it to go deeper into each vital sign.

Scores above 23 indicate your group is doing great in that vital sign!

If your group scores between 23 and 30 for all the vital signs, you're healthy! Encourage your core team members to find a core team of their own and start a new group when they're ready, and keep up the great work.

APPENDIX F

LAUNCHING A HEALTHY NEW GROUP

How can you launch a new group so it is healthy from the start? If I may be so bold, I believe you are blessed to be reading this book now, before heading down a path that may lead to unhealthy group practices. Utilizing the principles found here, you can start well and finish strong.

Vital Sign #1: LAUNCHING A NEW, CHRIST-CENTERED GROUP

As I said at the beginning of Chapter 1, God arranges the parts of the group the way he wants them to be. So you must start there. Who will be the first member of the group? Christ. You start with him at the center. As I discussed in Chapter 2, your main job as a leader is to stay close to him.

Start with your relationship with Christ Jesus. If you are not already spending time in his presence, depending on his power, and living out his purposes, don't invite any other humans to join you just yet! Abide in him. Spend some solitary time with him. Pray. Ask him about his purposes for you and this group. Don't rush this process, because it is all about him.

When you sense Christ's calling to launch a group, begin by asking him whom else he wants you to invite. Specifically, petition him daily to put the right people in your path and give you the spiritual eyes to know them when you see them. Trust in his leadership and authority. To be clear, this does not mean to passively sit around and wait for people to come to you. As Christ's ambassador (2 Corinthians 5:20), you should be active in looking for people, putting yourself in social situations where you might meet people in your neighborhood, on ball fields, playgrounds, workplaces, and anywhere else God places you. Christ will draw people to himself and therefore to you (see John 6:44 for this principle displayed in Jesus' own life). So get ready!

Randall Neighbour provides some great diagrams contrasting unhealthy vs. healthy group formation:[1]

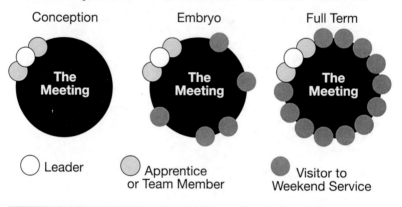

"Herding" new members into groups fosters a meeting mentality, which may never become relational and Christ-centered:

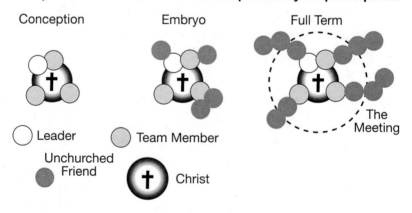

Relying upon Christ-centered, organic group formation produces more personal transformation and responsibility for participants:

In these illustrations, an unhealthy group finds its identity in a meeting. A healthy, Christ-centered small group gathers around the presence of Christ. Notice how the group forms. It doesn't start with twelve people who put their names on a list to get connected in a group. No, it launches with a leader who is connected intimately with Christ; who then develops a core team as Christ draws them; who then invites other friends to the group. This process is dependent on Christ's leadership.[2]

Vital Sign #2: LEADING A HEALTHY NEW SMALL GROUP

As a new leader or even a veteran leader preparing to launch a new small group be sure—in the midst of your preparations—to spend a *lot* of time with the Father:

1. On your knees, clarify your calling is from God and not just from your pastor, the small groups point person at your church, other members of the group, or yourself. Ask the Father to confirm your calling. Seek out his heart for your leadership.

2. Ask God to work in you and through you as you prepare to lead. Surrender your leadership, the group, and all your preparations to him.

3. Ask him to send you your core team (discussed in Chapter 3). These are the team members with whom you will share leadership.

4. If you already have people in the group, pray for them individually every day. Make this a habit. Ask them how you can pray for them and then be faithful to do it.

5. Ask God to surprise you. Acknowledge that he can and will do more than you can ever imagine!

Vital Sign #3: HOW TO LAUNCH A NEW GROUP WITH A CORE TEAM

Here are the steps Jesus used to discover and develop his core team. Use the same steps to launch a healthy group.

1. Ask. If the group belongs to God and he is the real leader, where do you start to find your core team? The same place Jesus did: through prayer. Jesus did not go out and recruit his disciples. He apparently did not even have a job description and never interviewed anyone! His Father simply gave them to him. Begin by asking God to send you the people he wants to be part of your core team.

2. Wait and watch patiently. What you do after you pray is crucial. When you pray, expect that God will answer, but remember this important fact: the timing is his, not yours. This is vital for any group that will bear fruit: before doing anything else, prayerfully wait for God to move. Then keep your spiritual eyes and ears open for whom God will send you, no matter how long it takes.

3. *Meet with the core team God has provided.* Once God gives you two or three core team members, begin meeting with them to pray, plan, and wait on God to move. The core team may meet together for a week or two or several months. Remember that the timetable is God's and not yours. Many groups begin with just a few individuals or couples, whether they planned it that way or not. These leaders sometimes grow frustrated and feel like quitting because they had an expectation of having far more people in their groups. I remind them that God has given them a core team to invest in and with whom to share leadership. God will not give them more people if they will not invest into the few he's given them!

4. *Expand.* After praying and planning together, the core team is ready to invite people to join them. If they've learned to trust God and keep their eyes open, the core team members usually find that God has already put the right people in their paths in their neighborhoods, at other church activities, in their families, workplaces, and other social activities (like their kids' sporting events).

Over the years I've observed many solo leaders who were the only ones who "recruited" people to the group. This is inefficient and often ineffective. In a healthy group, the core team takes ownership right away by praying and then inviting people in their spheres of relationship into the group. This act is also vital for how group members will be shepherded and discipled in the future. Relational discipleship and shepherding happen naturally among the people core team members have invited.

5. *Launch.* With the core team, launch the group, sharing leadership with them and sharing ownership with the entire group.

I highly recommend launching a new group by using *Launch into Community Life: Building a Master Plan of Action with a New Group*, a four-session group discussion guide I wrote with core-team leadership in mind (TOUCH Publications, 2008).

Some people who read *The Pocket Guide to Burnout-Free Small Group Leadership* have asked me about the difference between sharing ownership and sharing leadership of the group. I apparently did not make this distinction very clear in that book, so I'll clarify here:

> **Core team members share leadership.**
> **Everyone shares ownership.**

Core team members are not better than or "higher up" than other group members. Their role is to serve the group through their shared leadership. Jesus' core team members (Peter, James, and John) had a hard time understanding this. They thought their leadership roles in the group entitled them to higher positions, power, and privileges. Their leader had to remind them that to lead is to serve (See Mark 10:35-45).

And, here's the really cool thing: Over time, participants who share ownership grow to share leadership and become part of the core team. As the group grows numerically and spiritually, core team members form their own core teams and naturally step out together to launch new groups. This isn't just theory. In the few churches I know who are using core team leadership (including Northeast), groups are healthy, growing, and multiplying naturally (without being asked).

Vital Sign #4: LAUNCHING A NEW SMALL GROUP WITH PROACTIVE LEADERSHIP

Much of Chapter 4 was written with current groups in mind. Many of them are unhealthy because they never developed goals and plans together. Don't make that same mistake. I wrote *Launch into Community Life* specifically for new small groups to develop their goals and plans. I used the beginning of the Book of Acts as an example to follow in launching a healthy and life-changing ministry. The best thing: it's just four sessions, so you can work through it quickly as you launch.

Vital Sign #5: LAUNCHING A NEW GROUP
THAT LIVES IN AUTHENTIC COMMUNITY

My old friend and mentor, Lyman Coleman, says, "You have to become a group first, and then you are ready to get involved in discipleship and serving together. He's right. As you start a new group, be sure to spend a lot of time sharing together and getting to know one another. As you do, you'll find that spiritual growth and serving comes more naturally. A great resource for this is *Connecting Inward: Helping your group members develop a deep love for one another*, by Mark Collins (TOUCH Publications, 2005).

Vital Sign #6: LAUNCHING A MISSIONAL GROUP

A healthy small group is missional from the beginning. Even as you build authentic community with one another within the group, you fulfill Christ's mission by being open to others, praying for people in your spheres of influence who do not have a relationship with Christ, and watching for opportunities to serve. When your group is ready to do so, use *Reaching Outward: Helping your group members bring Christ into everyday relationships*, by Jim Egli (TOUCH Publications, 2005).

Vital Sign #7: LAUNCHING A NEW DISCIPLE-MAKING GROUP

The ten vital discipleship factors for small groups that I shared in Chapter 7 are as appropriate for new groups as existing ones—and much easier to implement! All the other vital signs build the environment and provide everything needed to be a life-changing group. From the beginning, however, be intentional about implementing those discipleship factors … and don't forget that the Holy Spirit—not you, not a curriculum, not a discipleship study, not a program—is the agent of spiritual growth. I wrote *Moving Forward: Helping your group members embrace their leadership potential* (TOUCH Publications, 2005) to help groups focus on spiritual growth that leads to leadership development.

A GUIDE TO MOVE YOUR GROUP TOWARD
"YESHIVA" DISCIPLESHIP

Use this brief guide to help your group become a disciple-making small group just like Jesus' *yeshiva*. You might want to walk through this first as a core team, and then with the entire group.

Begin by helping the group to "confront the brutal facts." Is discipleship happening in your group? Why not? Use open-ended questions such as these:

- How would you define *discipleship?*
- How do you think Jesus' disciples would define *discipleship?*
- What do you think discipleship would look like for us?
- What kinds of things do you need to grow in your relationship with God?

Read passages on discipleship such as Luke 14:25-35; John 15:12-17; or John 17:6-19, and lead a discussion about what a disciple is. As you lead, be sure to guide (but don't force) the discussion gently using some of the points in the process discussed in Chapter 7. Help the group to discover what real discipleship is. Another good passage to read is the Great Commandment: Matthew 22:34-40. Ask questions like:

- What can we learn from this passage about being a healthy small group?
- What are the most vital values?
- What does this passage teach us about discipleship?

To begin to move the group toward *implementing* a more healthy process for discipleship, ask questions such as these, designed to move you into planning and some goal setting:

- In one year, where do you see your walk with God? How does it look different than today? How about two years? Five?
- In one year, where do you see our group as far as being a discipling environment? How about two years? Five?
- Since Jesus gave us our commission to "go and *make* disciples," what does that imply for our group? How do we fulfill his commission?
- How will we measure success with discipleship? How do we know if we are actually doing it?

One of the main ways we can measure discipleship success is by looking at leader reproduction and eventual group multiplication. When disciples are being produced; when people are growing in their faith in God; when people are moving from being fed to feeding themselves to feeding others, the natural result is new leaders!

Preface

1. http://homepage.mac.com/christschurch/Blog/files/3678371b3f9e08a288099223fe29ce83-10.html
   http://jamesryle.blogspot.com/2008/09/healthy-things-grow.html

Introduction

1. Warren Wiersbe, Bible Exposition Commentary of the Old Testament: Prophets, for Amos 5:14-15, in WordSearch 7 (2007, WordSearch Corp.)
2. Ralph W. Neighbour, Jr. discusses this subject thoroughly in *Christ's Basic Bodies*, especially Chapter 4 (Houston: TOUCH Publications, 2008).
3. Jim Collins, Good to Great (New York: Harper Collins, 2001), 1.
4. M. Scott Boren, *The Relational Way* (Houston: TOUCH Publications, 2007), 244.
5. Chip Ingram, *Good to Great in God's Eyes* (Baker Books, 2007), 140.
6. Northeast Christian is a large church with many small groups and hundreds of first-time visitors every month. During this season of small group health examination, we did launch new small groups, but we didn't aggressively pursue small group ministry expansion. We sought to strategically launch fewer, but much healthier groups and leverage our focus on group health in existing groups so those groups could multiply naturally and make room for visitors.
7. The healthiest of our groups have not only multiplied but do so regularly, usually about once or twice per year. This is not the norm yet, however. Transforming groups to good health and great vitality takes time, effort, and risk-taking faith. Because so many Christians settle for ordinary, this transition does not happen overnight.

Chapter 1

1. http://www.ccci.org/how-to-know-god/would-you-like-to-know-god-personally/index.htm.
2. This problem is partially a doctrinal issue. Jesus Christ is seen as a human with a little divinity inside him when he needed it. But Christ is literally and infinitely more than that! He made what commentators usually call "preincarnate" appearances throughout the Old Testament age, meeting personally with Hagar, Abraham, Moses, Balaam, Gideon, Elijah, and others. He met with and delivered Shadrach, Meshach, and Abednego inside a fiery furnace (Daniel 3:25). He appeared in Zechariah's dream on a red horse standing among the myrtle trees. He was there, standing in the midst of them, watching over his people (Zechariah 1:8, ff.).
3. This concept comes from an article by Henri Nouwen, "Moving from Solitude to Community to Ministry," *Leadership*, Spring 1995. (Online at http://www.ctlibrary.com/le/1995/spring/5l280.html).
4. Nouwen.
5. Here's how I teach groups to pray recognizing Christ's presence with us: we share our needs and "supplications" to one another and Christ at the same time. I purposely have not created a bunch of rules or strict guidelines for this. Some people close their eyes and lift up their concerns in a traditional prayer pattern while others make their requests known in a more conversational style, sharing with everyone, including Christ. I do ask the members to keep their prayers short and as conversational as possible. We're learning to pray for one another's needs as we go along. So, for instance, Chris prays for his neighbor who does not know Christ, and then Rich jumps in and prays for the man's wife and family as well, then Donna join in and asks God to give Chris an opportunity to share with his neighbor. Then Dennis tells all of us about a work colleague who was in a car accident. Then Felicia thanks God that Dennis was able to comfort his work friend.
6. Warren Wiersbe, *Bible Exposition Commentary of the New Testament*.

Chapter 2

1. I first discussed the principle in *Leading from the Heart* (TOUCH Publications, 2001), using King David as an example of a leader after God's own heart. In *I'm a Leader . . . Now What?* (Standard Publishing, 2007) I showed how Jesus is the "best small group leader ever," and explored the attributes of his leadership that made him a great leader. Then, in *The Pocket Guide to Burnout-Free Small Group Leadership* (TOUCH Publications, 2009), the first words of the book exposed the truth that God is the *real* leader and that your job is to "lead from the second chair."

2. If you would like to find out how to invite Christ into your life and do not have someone to ask right now, go to http://www.ccci.org/how-to-know-god/index.htm. You should still seek out a Christ-follower to talk to as well, even if you do go to a web site for help.

3. Warren Wiersbe, *Bible Exposition Commentary of the Old Testament.*

4. Sanders, 36.

5. Collins, 21.

6. I go into much more detail about the calling to leadership in *Leading from the Heart* (TOUCH Publications, 2001), Chapter 4: "The Heart of the Call."

7. See Chapter 2 of *Leading from the Heart* and Chapter 4 of *I'm a Leader . . . Now What?* (Standard Publishing, 2007).

8. I go into much more detail about servant-leadership in my other books, especially *I'm a Leader . . . Now What?,* Chapter 5.

9. In his book, *Prepare Your Church for the Future,* Carl George lists 50 small group leadership topics for the "skill" portion of leader training meetings (142, 143). While the topics he lists are all good ones, producing such a list would only serve to overwhelm leaders.

10. Ben Reed, *Life & Theology: Thoughts on How I See the World,* http://www.benreed.net/index.php/2010/12/04/good-small-groups.

Chapter 3

1. While it seems that Andrew was not included as much in Jesus' inner circle as the other three, he was included at least once when the two sets of brothers pulled Jesus aside privately to ask him some questions (Mark 13:4). Interestingly, when the Gospel writers listed the Twelve, Matthew and Luke list the brothers together: Peter and Andrew, then James and John. But Mark separates the sets of brothers, placing Andrew fourth on the list behind Peter, James, and John. In the listing of the eleven apostles in Acts 1:13, Luke places them in this order: Peter, John, James, and then Andrew. Is there any significance to this? We can only surmise, but the order of names in a list was usually very significant in Jewish culture.

2. Leroy Eims, *The Lost Art of Disciple Making* (Grand Rapids, MI: Zondervan, 1978), 45, 46.

3. We witness numerous one-on-one conversations between Jesus and Peter in the gospels. Jesus even appeared personally to Peter after the resurrection (Luke 24:34; 1 Corinthians 15:5). Of course one of the most notable conversations between Jesus and Peter occurred on the shores of the Sea of Galilee, where Jesus gave Peter his threefold restoration and personal commission (John 21:15-19). After Jesus' ascension, Peter became the obvious leader of the apostles and the early church (see Acts 1:15, ff.; 2:14, ff.; 4:8, ff.), thus becoming what Jesus had prepared him for. Perhaps this is why Peter is always named first in every list of the apostles.

4. Quoted on *The Naked Truth about Small Groups* blog, www.randallneighbour.com, January 18, 2010.

5. Dr. Bill Donahue, "Why Leaders Don't Share Leadership," December 6, 2010. http://drbilldonahue.com/2010/12/why-leaders-dont-share-leadership. I have used Donahue's list; the explanations for each are mine.

6. Ken Blanchard, Bill Hybels, and Phil Hodges, *Leadership by the Book* (New York: William Morrow and Company, 1999), 70.

7. I discuss this in much more detail in Chapter 4 of *The Pocket Guide to Burnout-Free Small Group Leadership.*

Chapter 4

1. Andy Stanley and Bill Willits, *Creating Community* (Sisters, Oregon: Multnomah Publishers, 2004), 51-53.

2. Henry T. and Melvin D. Blackaby, *A God-Centered Church: Experiencing God Together* (Nashville, Tennessee: Broadman and Holman Publishers, 2007), 85.

3. Collins, Ch. 4.

4. Ibid., 88.

5. I will not go into detail here about how to do a S.W.O.T. analysis in your group. There are several websites that describe this thoroughly. One that is particularly good without being too detailed is at http://www.planonline.org/planning/strategic/swot.htm.

6. Stanley and Willits, 57.

7. Stanley and Willits, 65.

8. For more on SMART goals:
   http://www.goal-setting-guide.com/smart-goal-setting-a-surefire-way-to-achieve-your-goals
9. If you happen to read any old articles by me on the Internet on this topic, yes, I've changed my mind considerably over the years of leading groups!

Chapter 5

1. Nouwen, "Moving from Solitude to Community to Ministry."
2. Gilbert Bilezikian, *Community 101:Reclaiming the Local Church as Community of Oneness* (Grand Rapids, Michigan: Zondervan, 1997), 16-19.
3. For an in-depth study from these New Testament letters, see Romans 12:5; 1 Corinthians 12:12, 20; Galatians 3:28; Ephesians 2:14; 4:3-6; Philippians 1:27; 2:2; and Colossians 3:15.
4. Richard Peace, *Small Group Evangelism: A Training Program for Reaching Out with the Gospel* (Downers Grove, IL: InterVarsity Press, 1985), 67, 68.
5. The apostle John spoke about this in the beginning of his first letter. First, he invites his readers (including you and me) into fellowship, recognizing that this fellowship is only possible through the Father and his Son, Jesus Christ (1 John 1:3). Then he invites us to step out of the darkness of concealed sin. "If we claim to have fellowship with [God] yet walk in the darkness, we lie and do not live by the truth" (v. 6). Next he invites us to bring our sin into the light, which brings us into real, authentic community with one another and God: "But if we walk in the light, as he is in the light, we have fellowship with one another, and the blood of Jesus, his Son, purifies us from all sin" (v. 7). Next, he reminds us of the consequences of keeping our lives hidden from God and others: "If we claim to be without sin, we deceive ourselves and the truth is not in us" (v. 8). Finally, John invites us to bring our sin into the light through confession: "If we confess our sins, he is faithful and just and will forgive us our sins and will purify us from all unrighteousness" (v. 9). Confession allows us to have healthy community with one another. If we are hiding parts of ourselves in the darkness, we can't have real community with one another or real fellowship with God. None of us is without sin. If we claim something other than that, we are a group of liars and God's Word has no place in our lives (v. 10). As Christ-followers we are new creations in Christ and he has redeemed us by his blood, yet we are still in a daily spiritual battle. Later in his letter, John told his readers that "the Spirit who lives in you is greater than the spirit who lives in the world" (1 John 4:4). The word you in this verse is plural. He is addressing this to the community. We do not enter into this spiritual battle alone. As we face the daily fray, John encourages us to do this together, in genuine community. We do this best when we have developed trust, learned to share our stories, affirmed one another, confessed our weaknesses and failures, and when we are praying regularly with and for one another.
6. My favorite book on this subject is *Why Didn't You Warn Me? How to Deal with Challenging Group Members* by Pat Sikora. Visit Pat's website at http://whydidntyouwarnme.com.
7. Heather Zempel, "Community Is Messy, Part 2: Sweat," *Wineskins for Discipleship* blog, November 4, 2010.
8. Ibid.
9. Bill Donahue and Russ Robinson, *Building a Church of Small Groups* (Grand Rapids, Michigan: Zondervan, 2001), 58.

Chapter 6

1. Rick Rusaw and Eric Swanson, *The Externally Focused Church* (Loveland, Colorado: Group, 2004), 86.
2. The story is found in Luke 8:40-47.
3. Christian A. Schwarz, *Natural Church Development: A Guide to Eight Essential Qualities of Healthy Churches* (St. Charles, Illinois: Churchsmart Resources, 1996), 32.
4. Rusaw and Swanson, 122.
5. Alan Danielson blog post, "Enchi-fricken-ladas," October 12, 2010, http://www.3threat.net/2010/10/12/enchi-fricken-ladas.
6. Jim Petersen, *Living Proof* (Colorado Springs: NavPress, 1989), 120.
7. http://www.smallgroups.com/articles/2002/evangelisticprayer.html
8. Petersen, 126.
9. Petersen, 144.

Chapter 7

1. Jim Petersen, *Lifestyle Discipleship: The Challenge of Following Jesus in Today's World* (Colorado Springs: NavPress, 1993), 15.
2. Cartoon used by permission of Mary Chambers.
3. John Eldredge, *Waking the Dead* (Nashville: Thomas Nelson, 2003), 194.
4. Eldredge, 197.
5. From his book, *Discipleship*. Excerpted from the web site, http://www.ymresourcer.com/model/basics.htm.
6. Revelation 3:20. This passage is often used evangelistically—Jesus is knocking on the door of a lost person's heart, inviting him to accept Jesus as Savior. But this passage is written to the church, to people who already claim Christ as Savior. Jesus is inviting Christians into deeper fellowship—intimacy—with him.
7. It's important that groups help new people transition into the commitments the group has made to one another and to mutual discipleship. This is a huge paradigm change for most people in the West. At the same time, the group is unapologetic for their focus on growing in their relationships with Christ. When a new person joins an existing group, for example, I train our leaders to take time to share stories (history) and help the new person to enter into this environment of mutual discipleship.

Conclusion

1. See Genesis 1:22, 28; 8:17; 9:1, 7; 17:6. 20; 28:3; 35:11; 47:27; 48:4; Exodus 1:7; and many other instances.

Appendix B

1. Brian Jones, "Why Churches Should Euthanize Small Groups," *Christian Standard*, http://christianstandard.com/2011/01/why-churches-should-euthanize-small-groups.
2. We used the "Likiert scale" for our survey. This scale measures respondents' attitudes toward the given statements and is useful for measuring dimensions of group life that are otherwise very difficult to measure. On our 5-point scale, we used these descriptions:
   1. Strongly Disagree
   2. Disagree
   3. Neutral
   4. Agree
   5. Strongly Agree

We have changed the labels on our new survey, based on whether the respondent believes the statement is true or not. (See Appendix E for current labels used.)

Appendix F

1. A variant of this diagram appeared in a blog entry on "The Naked Truth About Small Group Ministry," http://www.randallneighbour.com/2009/10/organic-small-group-formation.html
2. To learn more about this, see my book, *The Pocket Guide to Burnout-Free Small Group Leadership* (Touch Outreach Ministries).

The Pocket Guide to Burnout-Free Small Group Leadership: How to Gather a Core Team and Lead from the Second Chair

If the only way you've done groups is with the leader/apprentice model, this little book will revolutionize your ministry! The key is moving small group leaders into the role of a point person for a core team of group members. Then, the core team then takes over the leadership of the group.
(120 p.) ISBN: 978-0-9825352-1-9

Leading from the Heart: A Small Group Leader's Guide to Passionate Ministry

Does your ministry need a spark? What you will learn in this book will renew your heart for people, help you refocus your priorities, and recharge your ministry as a small group leader. If you are tired and need a spiritual boost, this book will lead you to the source of life and deeper into the heart of God.
(152 p.) ISBN 978-1-8808283-5-9

Launch into Community Life: Building a Master Plan of Action with Your Small Group

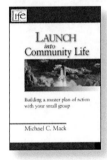

The four agendas will help you form a new group with a mission and vision and keep you—the leader—from burning out (utilizes the core team approach found in this book). Only one book per group required.
(64 p.) ISBN 978-0-9788779-5-8

Moving Forward: Helping Your Group Members Embrace Their Leadership Potential

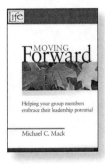

The six agendas will help your group members adopt a lifestyle of discipleship that takes them to the next levels of spiritual maturity. If your members are "stuck," this study will help them get going! Only one book per group required.
(72 p.) ISBN 978-0-9752896-7-9

Visit www.touchusa.org or call 800-735-5865 to order these resources directly from the publisher at a substantial savings off retail. Quantity discounts available.

NOTES

NOTES

NOTES